A LEGACY OF FORGIVENESS

The Story of
THOMAS EMMANUEL HERMIZ

JOHN WESLEY HERMIZ
in collaboration with
MARY ESTHER HERMIZ

Copyright © 2024 John Hermiz and Mary Esther Hermiz

ISBN: 978-1-953285-92-8

Published by Dust Jacket Press
A Legacy of Forgiveness: The Story of Thomas Emmanuel Hermiz / John Hermiz in collaboration with Mary Esther Hermiz

All rights reserved. No portion of this publication may be reproduced, stored in a retrieval system, or transmitted in any form or by any means, except for brief quotations in printed reviews, without prior permission of John Hermiz and Mary Esther Hermiz. Requests may be submitted by email: jhermiz8473@gmail.com

Dust Jacket Press
P.O. Box 721243
Oklahoma City, OK 73172

All Scripture quotations not otherwise designated are from The Holy Bible, English Standard Version. ESV® Text Edition: 2016. Copyright © 2001 by Crossway Bibles, a publishing ministry of Good News Publishers.

Permission to quote from the following additional copyrighted versions of the Bible is acknowledged with appreciation:

Holy Bible, New International Version®, NIV® Copyright ©1973, 1978, 1984, 2011 by Biblica, Inc.® Used by permission. All rights reserved worldwide.

The New King James Version® (NKJV). Copyright © 1982 by Thomas Nelson. Used by permission. All rights reserved.

Scripture quotations marked KJV are from the King James Version of the Bible.

Cover & interior design: D.E. West—www.zaqdesigns.com & Dust Jacket Creative Services

Printed in the United States of America

Blessed are you when others revile you
and persecute you and utter all kinds of evil against
you falsely on my account. Rejoice and be glad,
for your reward is great in heaven, for so they
persecuted the prophets who were before you.
(Matthew 5:11–12)

Repay no one evil for evil, but give thought to
do what is honorable in the sight of all. If possible,
so far as it depends on you, live peaceably with all.
Beloved, never avenge yourselves, but leave it to the
wrath of God, for it is written, "Vengeance is mine,
I will repay, says the Lord." To the contrary, "if your
enemy is hungry, feed him; if he is thirsty, give him
something to drink; for by so doing you will heap
burning coals on his head." Do not be overcome
by evil, but overcome evil with good.
(Romans 12:17–21)

CONTENTS

Prologue vii
Introduction ix

1. A Brief History 1
2. Life in Midyat 9
   (Early Twentieth Century) 9
3. The Hermiz Family 15
4. Lead-up to the Massacre 29
5. The Massacre of Midyat 39
6. Post-Massacre 47
7. Bound for America 57
8. Becoming Americanized 67
9. Becoming a Servant of the Lord 77
10. Travels to the "Old Country" 87
11. Seasoned Saint 95

Epilogue 97
Afterword 103
Appendix A 109
Appendix B 111
Appendix C 113

PROLOGUE

By John Hermiz

In 1934 Thomas E. Hermiz documented his early life experiences in a booklet titled *Mohammedan Persecution of Christians*. He later updated his story in a book titled *Trials and Triumphs of Thomas E. Hermiz*, a book that has now been out of print for many years. Since the last edition was published, additional information has surfaced from relatives and others who were themselves either survivors or descendants of those victimized by the Assyrian genocide of 1915. Their writings and various interviews have both validated and clarified those events.

Additionally, Bruce Farnham's 1985 book *My Big Father* and David Gaunt's 2006 work *Massacres, Resistance, Protectors: Muslim-Christian Relations in Eastern Anatolia During WWI* have been important resources for me in understanding the geopolitical landscape of this era. The writings of both authors have been very helpful toward providing some enlightenment as to the causes and the wider details of this conflict. If deeper understanding of these historical events is desired by the reader, we highly recommend these sources.

This book only scratches the surface of the many details leading to the massive genocide of both the Armenian and Assyrian people groups of the early twentieth century. And although an effort has been made to state the facts as accurately as possible, a scientific perfection is nearly impossible, as reliable documentation is scarce and much of the narrative is dependent on oral tradition provided by those who survived these atrocities.

In August 2012 I was privileged along with my son, Daniel, and two of my sisters, Ruthie and Mary Esther, to have the opportunity to visit the areas referenced in this book. We stayed in a five-star luxury hotel, a building that once belonged to our ancestors and was later occupied by the Turkish government and used for, among other things, sentencing a beautiful young woman (our grandmother) to a martyr's death. We have no desire to reclaim our family's property, but we do feel compelled to share the stories of the precious souls who once lived there.

It is with profound respect for our father and for his personal story that my sister Mary Esther and I have decided to humbly undertake the project of this rewrite. We are leaning heavily on dad's autobiographical writings as a baseline while attempting to enhance the original with additional background information received from others.

INTRODUCTION

Persecution has claimed the lives of literally millions of devoted followers of Jesus since the first-century stoning of Stephen (Acts 6). In that regard, this story may not be unique. The ethnic and religious assaults in the region of Mesopotamia that exploded in the early twentieth century have existed for hundreds and arguably thousands of years, and unfortunately they remain to the present day. But it is this story, this specific legacy, that has had a powerful impact on our lives. We hope in sharing it with you that you will be inspired and encouraged, and perhaps most importantly, be prepared for our day of persecution.

Thomas Emmanuel Hermiz was born April 7, 1911, in the ancient city of Midyat in present-day Turkey. Eventually Thomas emigrated to the United States, where he married, raised a family, and spent over sixty years in faithful Christian ministry. What makes his otherwise "ordinary" adult life nothing short of miraculous is the story of those early years. Thomas witnessed atrocities beyond imagination rooted in centuries-old religious and ethnic hatred and vengeance. The fact that he even survived the chaos and violence of his young life with his mind and body intact is the unmistakable result of God's grace and providence. This is his story.

There are many godly heroes in Dad's story—Thoma, his grandfather and the one we regard as the Christian patriarch of the family; Tirzah, his mother, who sacrificed life on earth rather than deny her love for Jesus; Agnes Fenenga, a Congregational missionary who was a key figure in his rescue; David Hood, a Sunday School teacher whose greatest impact in our father's life may have been simply that he "seemed to enjoy his religion"; and several others. We wish to honor them in the rewriting of Dad's story.

We are also intrigued by the several characters who in the providence of God also played an important role in his story but who by their own admission were not devoted followers of Christ—his father, Emmanuel; his Aunt Medjida; his adoptive Muslim mother, Fatima; and others. We feel compelled to give them their proper places as well, to give them the respect and appreciation they are due for loving Thomas well and for having been used by God in significant ways to rescue and bring healing to this broken and traumatized little boy.

Mostly, we desire to honor the Lord Jesus Christ, the one who orchestrated the entire story. It is to Him this work is dedicated.

1

A Brief History

ASSYRIANS LIVING IN MESOPOTAMIA

Thomas and all those in his immediate family of origin believed their ethnicity to be "100-percent Assyrian"; his forebearers even believed they were directly descended from Abraham, who the reader may remember lived in Ur of the Chaldees, a location thought by some to be very close to where Thomas grew up. Modern genetic technology might tell a different story. As anyone who has had an analysis performed of his or her DNA can testify, most all of us are a mix of multiple ethnicities. The history of the ancient term "Assyrian" as well as other related terms such as "Chaldean," "Nestorian," "Syriac," "Jacobite," and others is both complicated and hotly debated to this day by the academic community *and* on the Internet. The *Digest of Middle East Studies* well documents the many controversies of these related people groups without attempting to solve the various arguments.

Suffice to say that over thousands of years and countless wars, the land of Mesopotamia (land between the Tigris and Euphrates Rivers) has changed hands many times. Borders between nations have moved, languages have evolved, and one religion or another has supplanted the previous deeply held religious belief system. Being an ardent student of the Old Testament, Thomas frequently pointed out that the multitude of Middle East conflicts throughout history could be traced to the time of the patriarchs: Abraham, Isaac, and Jacob, especially highlighting the troubles of Jacob and Esau.

Many attempts over the last fifteen centuries have been made to eradicate the Christian faith from this region. But Christianity has not been blotted out, because as He has always done, God intervened time and time again to enable His bride to hold fast to her Redeemer. Many have been martyred, many more deported, but a remnant remain to this very day, and having been refined by the fires of persecution, they continue to stand, and the church of Jesus Christ in this little-known corner of the Middle East still flourishes.

For purposes of our story, it is most critical to note that for whatever his genetic code may have been, and for whatever details of his history might have been confused or unknown, one thing is certain—Thomas was the son of a woman whose love for Christ led her to die as a martyr rather than renounce her faith. That sense of heritage dramatically marked his life and the lives of those who would come after him.

OTTOMAN EMPIRE

For more than 600 years leading up to the time of Thomas's birth, the Islamic sultans ruled a very large geographical area that included Turkey and the land of Mesopotamia, which is modern Iraq, northeastern Syria together with southeastern Turkey, and western Iran. But by the time of our story, they had greatly devolved as a world power, as expressed in what had become a common descriptive phrase, "sick man of Europe."

In 1908, prior to the complete dismantling of the empire, a coalition of army officers, college students, and others forcefully crushed the power of the reigning sultan (Abdulhamid) and sought to reform the Ottoman government from within, referring to themselves as the "Young Turks." It was the Young Turks who in 1914 and 1915 directed Ottoman soldiers and their proxies to execute or deport hundreds of thousands of both Armenians and Assyrians. Estimates range as high as 1.5 million Armenians and anywhere from 300,000 to 750,000 Assyrians executed. Hundreds of thousands more were deported or left of their own accord. This has been well chronicled in the history books as the "Armenian genocide." The "Assyrian genocide" sometimes called "Seyfo" has received less attention but was just as brutal and is the backdrop of our story.

The Ottoman government's problem with the Armenians and the Assyrians had little to do with their ethnicities. What distinguished these two people groups from the rest of their Turkish countrymen was in fact their religion. As long as these predominantly Christian people groups kept to their own communities, their faith and customs were tolerated by the Sultans. The increasingly authoritarian Young Turks, however, suspicioned that these Christians had too many ties to Europe and the USA. They feared what they perceived as their disloyalty to the sovereignty of the Ottoman Empire. They made a strategic decision—Christianity did not belong in the Ottoman Empire; it was incompatible with Turkish nationalism; therefore, it would no longer be tolerated.

From 1913 to the end of World War I, the Young Turks set about to destroy any remnant of the Christian church within their borders. They were largely successful. Hundreds of thousands were killed and thousands more refugees from both ethnicities were in one manner or another forcibly uprooted from their homes and altogether removed from the region. After joining forces with Germany and the Central Powers in World War I and suffering humiliating defeat, the empire was dissolved by treaty and officially came to an end in 1922.

TURKISH HISTORY—ETHNIC AND RELIGIOUS

The nation known today as Turkey is essentially all that is left of the old Ottoman Empire. As such, it has long been made up of a multitude of ethnic groups such as Arabs, Kurds, Armenians, Assyrians, and numerous others. Although Islam was the official religion until the Turkish constitution was amended in 1924, it remains to this day as by far the dominant religion throughout the region. However, there are several branches of the Christian faith as well as Judaism and other religions that have coexisted and even thrived there for centuries.

For a couple of examples, fifteen miles to the southeast of Midyat, where our story takes place, stands to this day the Monastery of Mor St. Gabriel, which is the oldest surviving Syriac Orthodox monastery in the world, dating back to the fourth century. And approximately fifty miles to the southwest of Midyat is the town of Mardin, home to a church that adherents claim was planted in the first century by Timothy, the mentee of the apostle Paul.

The seven churches referenced in Revelation to whom Jesus wrote letters are all geographically located in what is today western Turkey. And the ancient city of Antioch, where believers were first called "Christians," exists today as Antakya in southern Turkey. Over the centuries the town of Midyat in southeastern Turkey became known as a haven for many Christian families who had fled oppression in other regions. Whole large clans of Christian refugees sought refuge there.

Most of the cities and villages in the region around Midyat were heavily populated by loyal followers of Islam. In this regard, Midyat was unique in that most of its population claimed Christianity as their religion. Some were Chaldean Catholic, some Protestant, many more were Syriac Orthodox (also known as "Jacobite"), but even with their diverse doctrinal distinctives, they had more in common with each other than they did with their Muslim counterparts.

History records that from time to time, acts of violence have been committed by Christians against Muslims. We submit that these were done in direct disobedience to our Lord's commands—there is no biblical support for such hostile activity. Committed Christians are required by Scripture—"So far as it depends on you, live peaceably with all" (Romans 12:18). And Jesus said, "All who take the sword will perish by the sword" (Matthew 26:52).

Muslims, on the other hand, are guided by a charge from the Quran to engage in Jihad (holy war) against those of other faiths. Obviously not all Muslims are terrorists, but some accurately point to passages where the Quran instructs them to dominate the world by any means necessary. Inevitably, due to that instruction and the example set by the prophet Muhammad in the seventh century, peace has always been elusive at best. As much as we wish to regard the majority of Muslims in the modern world as a generally peaceful people, they have a long history of forcing conversions, imposing their faith on the willing and unwilling alike.

The harsh reality is that well before the massacre of 1915 (the focus of our story), Christians were regarded as second-class citizens by most in the country and were often targeted and persecuted by the much larger Muslim population. The Nomadic Kurds were a constant threat to their security. The early twentieth century was not the first time, nor would it be the last, when a handful of zealous leaders from one party or another would decide that a pluralistic society was not in alignment with the goals of Turkish culture.

2

Life in Midyat
(Early Twentieth Century)

A MIDDLE EASTERN COMMUNITY

Midyat was the capital of the villages in a region referred to as Tur Abdin, a large plain surrounded by tree-covered hills and encircled by orchards and vineyards. On the eve of World War I, various sources report a total population of approximately 8,000 people, most of whom spoke Assyrian, a modern version of the ancient Aramaic. In the early twentieth century, a few cobblestone streets were outnumbered by the many dirt roads, which were very difficult to navigate, especially in winter.

Just outside the city limits the residents raised livestock and produced grains such as wheat and barley, just as their ancestors had done for thousands of years. Throughout the city itself, walnut trees, fig trees, and grape vines were scattered somewhat sparsely. Figs, raisins, olives, and hazelnuts were widely available.

A LEGACY OF FORGIVENESS

As common as rice in southeast Asia or corn in America, bulgur was the mainstay of the typical Assyrian's diet. This form of wheat is cracked, steamed, dried, then prepared in numerous ways, such as when combined with other ingredients like lemon oil and cucumber in the popular "tabbouleh" salad. Rolled grape leaves stuffed with lamb and rice were a common staple in most of the Mediterranean countries, each region seasoning to suit their local taste preferences. In Midyat this dish was called "yabra." Yogurt was another favorite homemade dish.

The houses were made of stone, built on rock foundations, and were separated only by common concrete walls between them. Many of the actual living quarters were elevated (think second floor) with animals such as sheep, goats, and turkeys kept on the ground level. Thomas could remember trying to climb the exterior stone walls of his home even as a very young child, generally without success and bearing the scars to prove it! His older cousins remembered the thrill of jumping from one flat rooftop to another.

Houses behind walls on Midyat street

Animals kept on ground floor of living quarters

A LEGACY OF FORGIVENESS

In this semi-arid environment it was not unusual for families to sleep on their roofs during the very hot summers. Beds on the rooftops had to be elevated to avoid crickets and scorpions, which inhabited the area. Electricity had not yet come to southeast Turkey, so sundown was the unofficial bedtime. The Hermiz family cousins recounted many warm family times when after dark the adults and children would gather around a lantern, enjoy great conversation, and maybe do some reading or crocheting—rich memories of happier days. In winter all of them would sleep in one room heated with wood.

The blue furniture on the roofs is raised beds.

Some of the Hermiz men wore Western-style clothing, but most of them dressed like their fellow countrymen: Arab-style dresses or gowns cinched with a cloth belt. Women and children wore similar Middle Eastern-style flowing dresses. Leather was brought in from Syria, and local shoemakers would design and cobble their footwear.

The "fez" was the main headdress for Christian and Jewish men. Otherwise, Arab and Kurdish men wore the "keffiyeh," the traditional turban-style headdress worn by men in most parts of the Middle East since at least the seventh century.

CONGREGATIONAL MISSIONARIES

Throughout the nineteenth century, European and American missionaries were held in high regard by the Ottoman government as well as by the populace because they were known as men and women of principle, quick to help any community in need. Their willingness to educate and to serve the medical needs of the people was enough for the Muslim leaders to tolerate their Christianity, especially in the more rural parts of the empire. Unfortunately, such tolerance came with an expiration date.

The Congregational Church of New England sent missionaries to the region in the mid-1800s, forming a base of operations in the city of Mardin, some fifty miles to the west of Midyat, seeking to evangelize those who needed to hear the gospel of Jesus Christ.

Eventually the mission opened a boarding school, a medical work, and by necessity, expanded to include an orphanage. As our story unfolds, this operation will come to play a major role in the life of Thomas and several of his cousins.

For many years this Protestant mission experienced very little success in convincing the local population to embrace Christianity. Bruce Farnum's book tells the story of one of the pioneer missionaries to the area who wrote of being met with suspicion and antagonism to the extent that he was often spat upon, and at least once even stoned. Under the rule of the Islamic Ottomans, if any Muslim departed from the religion of Islam and converted to Christianity, or to any other religion for that matter, he faced certain persecution, being disowned by his family, and possibly execution. These conditions made for a very "hard soil" in which to plant seeds of the gospel of Jesus.

MISS AGNES FENENGA

One particular missionary had, as will become evident in the telling of Thomas's story, a critical role in his young life. Agnes Fenenga, a native of Pennsylvania, went to the mission field in 1901. By 1912, when tensions and conflicts were on the rise in the area, she had become principal of the girls' boarding school in Mardin. At the same time, she did general evangelistic work with the local women, which made her a regular visitor in Midyat.

Just prior to the massacre of 1915, the Turkish military forced her, along with two additional missionaries, to vacate the work in Mardin, and they were promptly moved to Constantinople (Istanbul). The residents of Mardin and Midyat strongly protested her removal, and with a sense that her work was not done, she chose not to return to the United States. After approximately one year of her forced exile, she was allowed to return to her ministry in Mardin.

As a result of the ravages of war, the role of the school became more important than ever. Not only was Agnes able to care for the needs of the many orphaned children, but she was also able to effectively advocate to the government on behalf of the many surviving Christian parents whose children were taken from them. These children had fallen into the hands of Muslim families, who were all too happy to raise them and indoctrinate them in the ways of Islam. The survival of many children was due to the devotion of this godly woman and others like her.

Agnes Fenenga

3

The Hermiz Family

AN ASSYRIAN FAMILY

The Hermiz* family tree can factually be traced back to 1800 to the city of Mosul, at that time in the southernmost part of old Mesopotamia, now modern Iraq (see appendix A). The reader may recall that Mosul is the site of old Nineveh, capital of the ancient Assyrian Empire and the site of the prophet Jonah's evangelistic efforts. In the early 1800s Eliya Hermiz moved his family from Mosul 160 miles northwest to Midyat, in northern Mesopotamia, which today is southeastern Turkey. Oral tradition states that the Hermiz family of Mosul came to Midyat bringing with them "bags of gold." It is thought that due to religious persecution throughout the region, this family of significant wealth and influence chose to relocate to Midyat, known widely as "the meeting point of religions and cultures."

*For the sake of consistency, I have chosen to use the Americanized spelling "Hermiz" throughout, although some of the men and women referenced in this story would have used an Assyrian/Chaldean variant, "Hirmiz."

Eliya Hermiz moved his family from Mosul, Iraq, to Midyat, Turkey.

Due to their inherited wealth and prosperity, some of the Hermiz men were (to say it politely) men of leisure, not feeling the need to generate an income. Others became farmers or herders. Quite a few of them went into business, being merchants mostly, with retail shops in Midyat. A few were importers. More than one went into politics, such as Galle Hermiz, who served eight years as the first mayor of the city, and Jacob Hermiz, who served as both a judge and a senator.

THOMA'S STORY

Our family owes a great debt of gratitude to the American missionaries for reasons that will become clearer as we continue the story. But no doubt the most important reason has to do with the story of Thoma Hermiz, who was Thomas's grandfather. Up to the time that Thoma was in his twenties, our understanding is that most everyone in the Hermiz family belonged to the Jacobite sect, also known as Syrian Orthodox.

For several years in the latter part of the 1800s, especially during the summer months, brave and devoted missionaries held open-air services in the marketplace of Midyat, gaining a wider hearing for the gospel among all the residents of the city. Thoma had been warned by his parents never to listen to these missionaries for fear that he would become "polluted in the sight of God." Although he was a young man with a wife and two children, he faithfully followed his parents' instruction; when he would pass by at the time they were holding services, he could be seen with his fingers in his ears.

On one occasion he was detained across the street from where the missionaries were ministering, and as he had done many times before, he dutifully placed his fingers in his ears to close out any sound of music or speaking. He was close to the open-air meat market, which of course attracted many flies. Repeatedly Thoma found it necessary to remove his fingers from his ears to swat the flies away. But in one instance that can be explained only as the providence of God, his ears were open long enough to hear the missionary quote the text *He that hath an ear, let him hear what the spirit saith* (Revelation 2:7 KJV).

Regardless of whether the missionary realized what

the young man was doing and quoted the text for his benefit, or just spoke the text to get the attention of all, the Spirit of God gripped Thoma in that moment and he decided to pay attention to what the missionary was saying. To the best of our knowledge, there is no record of exactly what the missionary said over the next few minutes. But in the continued reading of scripture and any additional commentary that might have been offered, Thoma quickly became convinced that something significant was missing from the religious tradition in which he had been raised.

Maybe it was the message of justification by faith. Maybe it was the emphasis on grace for salvation as opposed to good works. Maybe it was the knowledge that Thoma could experience a personal relationship with Jesus. Years later, grandson Thomas summed up the experience with this phrase: "As the missionary continued to talk and read from the Scriptures, the Holy Spirit opened that which had been closed to him previously."

Once converted, Thoma immediately experienced severe persecution. His parents completely disowned him for abandoning the Jacobite faith, and to the best of our knowledge they were never reconciled to him. Viewed as a heretic, he was beaten by his brother, and his father threatened to have him thrown into jail. Initially his wife wouldn't go near him or allow him to see his children. But he was committed and patient. Thankfully, after some period of separation, the relationships with his wife and children were restored. Over time he was reconciled to most of his family—and many of them, thanks to his faithful witness and the testimony and teaching of the missionaries, also became true followers of Christ.

Thoma quickly became a devout follower of Jesus. Over the next twenty years he became one of the most influential Christians in the city of Midyat, as well as one of the most prosperous. It became his passion to introduce others to a personal relationship with God through Jesus Christ. He opened several retail stores, and each time he opened a store he would take time to speak to his employees about the way of salvation. He became an avid student of the Bible and used that knowledge as a means of witnessing to others about the truth of Christ's provision.

Thoma's conversion seemed to spark a turning point, a breakthrough of sorts, in that the seeds that had been planted over several decades in people's hearts throughout the area began taking hold. Many converts were made, and a strong Bible-believing community began to form in the city. As a wealthy businessowner, Thoma was able to offer significant financial assistance to the American missionaries, and together they established a Congregational mission in Midyat. Years later, after Thoma's death, that same growing Protestant church had need of a building, and in 1912 construction began on a structure that stands to this day as a testimony to the faith of those early converts.

A LEGACY OF FORGIVENESS

Bethel Church

From the rooftop restaurant where we dined one pleasant evening in the summer of 2012, it was a particular blessing to look out over that ancient city, and amid the many minarets we could plainly see just a few blocks away the cross that still adorns the steeple of this lone Protestant church building, which is called Bethel. Ironically, the slight hill on which the church was built is the highest point in the city, making that cross easily visible to all.

Thoma lived to be only forty years old, but amazingly, that was long enough to see a few of his ten children married by the time he died in 1895. He had been ill for some time, and it seems that Thoma had a premonition as to the approximate time of his passing. He called his family about him, had them sing hymns and gospel songs, then like a prophet out of the Old Testament, he covered himself with a quilt upon his bed and without warning passed into the presence of the Lord. It was reported that his funeral was very well attended by Muslims and Christians alike, as he was highly respected by all in the community.

JACOB'S STORY

By all accounts, Thoma and his wife, Bessie, had a very close family. Without a doubt, each of the children had his or her own interesting and challenging personal story. We will spend some time exploring the life of his son Emmanuel, who was Thomas's father. But first we would like to honor another of Thoma's sons, Jacob.

As could be said of all of Thoma's children, despite the growing tensions in southeastern Turkey in the early 1900s, Jacob would say that he had a good life. He was a well-educated, well-to-do aristocratic gentleman living in a lovely home with his beloved family whose life was centered around the local Protestant church. He was able to read, write, and speak several languages but primarily used his native tongue of Assyrian, which was a form of the old Aramaic, the language of Jesus. As was the custom of the day in Turkey, Jacob married young with the intention of raising a large family. His faith and dedication to helping people led him to serve locally as an arbitrator (judge) and nationally as an elected senator. He considered himself a very blessed man.

However, the unrest in Turkey was significant, and although he held a responsible position in the community, he knew that the situation throughout the region was extremely volatile. It was becoming painfully clear with each passing day that the environment was becoming less and less conducive to raising a Christian family safely and securely. The American missionaries with whom Jacob was closely aligned encouraged him to consider relocating his family to the United States, where the Industrial Revolution was thriving, and more importantly where he would no longer have to face the kind of persecution that was becoming pervasive in his homeland.

After much consideration, Jacob made the decision to travel to America for the purpose of checking things out for himself. His thinking was that perhaps he could at the very least visit this land of freedom that he had read and heard so much about, then return to his family. Or better yet, he could possibly establish himself in the United States with a job and a place to live and then send for his family to join him. The missionaries connected him with a Congregational pastor in Central Falls, Rhode Island, and before long he was on his way to a new life in America. He was the first Hermiz male to immigrate to America, but he would not be the last. Over the next two years two of his younger brothers, Emmanuel and Alexander, joined him.

Life in America was very different for the Hermiz men. No longer could they enjoy a life of luxury and leisure. They had to cook for themselves and learn to run a household, something males in Turkey never did. But they found honor and dignity learning to work with their hands in textile mills and steel mills in the ensuing years. And the freedom to practice their religion without fear made it all worthwhile. Almost half the population in Central Falls were recent immigrants—English, Irish, Polish, Syrian, Assyrian, and others. Jobs were plentiful and the brothers quickly landed work in a local silk-weaving mill.

Sadly, Jacob, Alexander, and Emmanuel were never able to send for all their family members. Before those arrangements could be made, the town of Midyat was seized by the Kurds and most of their family members were either murdered, kidnapped, or died from exposure and disease in the aftermath of the massacre. A few of Jacob's children were placed in the orphanage in Mardin and in future years would rejoin their father in Central Falls.

EMMANUEL'S STORY

Jacob's brother (and Thomas's father) Emmanuel grew up in this atmosphere of constant persecution of Christians long before the Midyat massacre and witnessed terrible atrocities. Sadly, to the best of our knowledge Emmanuel never made the personal commitment to Christ that his father and other family members had. In fact, he learned to hate all Muslims in general and the Turks in particular. While his father lived, Thoma was able to restrain his son's hostilities, but once the family patriarch passed away, Emmanuel could not be held back in his efforts to seek vengeance against those whom he regarded as his enemies.

Some considered admirable his sense of justice and his actions that followed; others thought of him as more of a vigilante. Either way, some friends joined him in the fight, and together this "band of brothers" wreaked their own kind of havoc in the area surrounding Midyat. His quest for retribution resulted in his being branded as an outlaw. Soon the Turkish authorities were hunting him down, having placed a price for capture on his head.

Numerous friends warned him that he should probably leave the country or he would soon be captured and killed. Not one to run from a fight, he resisted at first, but having almost been captured a couple of times, he decided it might be prudent to listen to his friends' advice. In 1912, as tensions and hostile actions increased in the area, Emmanuel decided that it would be in everyone's best interest for him to leave the country.

So with some similar but mostly different motivations than his older brothers, Emmanuel made plans for the long trip to America. It was not an easy decision to leave behind his wife and young children for an unknown period, but America offered an opportunity where the family's religion and ethnicity would not be confronted with such hatred and violence. As with Jacob and Alexander, he would be giving up his fortune and to a large extent the only cultural experience he had ever known, but the desire for freedom, religious and otherwise, trumped every other consideration.

Before Emmanuel left Mesopotamia, he committed to his mother-in-law in writing that he would continue providing enough kuros (Ottoman Empire money) to feed and otherwise care for his wife, Tirzah, and their two children.

This contract was written in Arabic and stamped by four witnesses. Interestingly, the English translation of that document that we hold in our possession makes the statement that the four witnesses were "famous and rich." The Hermiz men would never again experience personally or rub shoulders with those of such fame or wealth.

Methods of travel were very crude in those days; one could travel across land only on foot or ride a horse, mule, or donkey. It is not known exactly how long it took Emmanuel to make the trip to America. It would have taken at least two weeks by horseback to get to Istanbul. From there, standard procedure was to sail across the Mediterranean to France. We know that he initially went to Brazil for perhaps as long as two years before finally disembarking at the port city of Providence, Rhode Island, joining his brothers in Central Falls.

We've also learned that the final leg of his journey from Brazil to America was interrupted. We are uncertain of exact dates, but it would have been shortly after World War I commenced in 1914. The ship that was transporting Emmanuel was stopped by the British Navy just off the coast of Barbados. There were a number of Germans aboard the transport ship whom the English determined were not going to be given passage to America. As previously mentioned, Turkey was allied with the Germans for purposes of the war, so Emmanuel was suspicioned to be in cahoots with them. Nothing could have been farther from the truth as Emmanuel hated the Turks. Nevertheless, he was incarcerated in Barbados for nine months before being processed and released to continue his journey and rejoin his brothers in Rhode Island. For reasons we are unsure of, Emmanuel later decided to move to Pittsburgh, where he would try his hand at being a salesman.

Three years after leaving Turkey, Emmanuel received word that all of his family had been massacred by the Kurdish Muslims. This wasn't entirely true, but it further embittered him against the Turks. So when President Woodrow Wilson and Congress declared war on Germany in April 1917, Emmanuel was among the first aliens to volunteer for the American Army. The fact that Turkey was aligned with Germany and the Central Powers was sufficient inducement for him to enlist.

Emmanuel served in General Pershing's 26th Yankee Division, specifically the 103rd field artillery. By all reports, he fought valiantly in southern France, earning for himself several decorations and medals, including the Distinguished Army Cross. Stories were circulated about his unorthodox but very effective prowess against the enemy, stories that can't be verified at this point, but suffice it to say that he displayed unusual bravery and earned the respect of his fellow soldiers and commanding officers. As with so many other World War I veterans, the effects of having been "gassed" in the line of duty would haunt him physically and mentally for the rest of his life. As a result of his enlistment, he was given naturalization and lived out the rest of his days as a proud and patriotic American citizen.

A LEGACY OF FORGIVENESS

Emmanuel Hermiz

We will pick up the story of Emmanuel in America after recapping the all-important events and the heart of our story, which took place in Midyat between 1914 and 1920.

4

Lead-up to the Massacre

REGIONAL JIHAD

We want to remind the reader that much of what follows is verifiable fact from data that can easily be validated with a quick Internet search. At the same time, we would be remiss not to point out that some of these statements and stories fall under the category of *assertions* made by eyewitnesses to their descendants. It is reasonable that we accept their claims and memories and that we remember and appreciate their trials, their tragedies, and their triumphs.

Even as the Ottoman Empire was imploding, Muslim jihad was exploding throughout southeast Turkey. Over a period of at least eighteen months there were multiple raids, most of which were initiated by the Kurds. It became inevitable that a massacre of hellish proportions was looming on the horizon. In the summer of 1914 the Ottoman government ordered mobilization, drafting men between the ages of twenty and forty-five to join the army, but few were enthusiastic. Residents of Midyat, where our story unfolds, reported later that some of the recruits from their city had to be taken away in chains. Few who were removed in this way ever returned.

The Ottoman government generally tolerated but had never been happy with any of the various branches of Christianity that existed in the territories they controlled; the powerful Young Turks were even less accommodating. Although the Turkish government of today still refuses to acknowledge the reality of the 1915 genocide, the evidence is abundantly clear that a strategic and well-planned attempt to eradicate Christianity from the region was initiated by the Young Turks. The Kurdish tribesmen who lived mostly in the mountains in and around the area were all too happy to collude with the official government forces to implement jihad. Their role could be accurately compared to Iran's Islamist proxies in the Middle East of today with such groups as Hamas and Hezbollah.

The gradual and systematic killing of Christians was planned early in the campaign, and the implementation of genocide took place in a well-organized and determined fashion. After the Turkish government and its Kurdish allies got rid of the Armenian Christians in each area, they would typically go after the Protestants, accusing them of supporting the Armenians and of having too much external contact with Western countries that were considered enemies of the Turkish state.

As 1915 began unfolding, Armenian and Assyrian Christians fleeing from massacres in Diyarbakir Province (an area in the Tigris River basin often referred to as the "Fertile Crescent") found their way to Midyat after crossing the mountains. Many described the killings and the persecution occurring in their villages. The people of Hasankeyf, the northernmost town with mixed Armenian and Assyrian populations, heard about these killings as well, so they sent several men to Midyat to investigate whether these reports were true.

They addressed their concerns to a visiting authority of the Ottoman government. According to some versions, this official had his daughter sitting on his lap at that meeting. He answered their expressed concerns this way: "Those rumors are as false as if I am committing incest with my own daughter." He stressed, "It is the Armenians who took up arms against the government, and the government for its part is taking measures to restore law and order."

Nevertheless, the arrival of considerable numbers of refugees in Midyat who had escaped from other villages that had been attacked by local Kurdish tribes did not cease. Nothing about these raids made sense if only the Armenians were to be punished. The leaders of Midyat were suspicious, but they had no clear idea of what to expect.

GALLE HERMIZ/HANNE SAFAR

Early in 1915 it became obvious that the situation for the Christians was growing more and more bleak. The mayor of Midyat during this time was Galle Hermiz, a prominent member of the Protestant Hermiz family and a popular politician who sat on the district and provincial advisory councils. Galle was a devoted Christian and a well-respected politician who seemingly lived above his ethnic and religious factions.

Before the general massacre in Midyat, Galle was informed that Christians were being killed in other cities and villages such as Edessa, Erzurum, Adana, Diyarbakir, and others. He called for a meeting with some of the other Christian leaders, discussing the need for unity among the various branches of the church to have any chance of effectively facing the imminent threat.

The Syriac Orthodox were led by a man named Hanne Safar. Hanne was so favored by the Sultan (Abdulhamid) that he had been officially awarded the honorary title of "Pasha" (General). The Sultan had awarded him official government decorations and medals and had honored him with a ceremonial sword.

Galle, Hanne, and the other religious leaders met in secret at Mort Shmuni Church. First they debated the issue of whether they should mount a resistance at all. Some, especially among the devout Protestants, felt that taking up arms, even in self-defense, was forbidden by Christ. Yet these very same men were torn, believing they had an obligation to protect their families. So they prayed together, searched the Scriptures, and counseled with one another. When all was said and done, most came to agreement, swearing on a Bible that they would stick together to mount a common defense.

When the government heard of this alliance, they summoned Hanne Safar to the town hall and explained that there must have been a misunderstanding. They admitted that Protestants and Catholics were targets since they had foreign connections. But they assured Hanne that the Syriac Orthodox would not be harmed because although not Muslim, their faith tradition was indigenous to the region. Hanne and the other leaders of the Syriac Orthodox Church in Midyat were lured into believing that their lives would be spared if they collaborated with the Young Turks to turn over the Protestant families.

Building on both class resentment and religious hatred, some Syriacs began arguing, "Why should we help the Hermiz clan, which is a large and rich family of Protestant converts who can defend themselves? What can be gained by involving us in the fate that is awaiting them?" Hanne Safar reversed his position after hearing this, took the government's bait, and told the Hermiz clan that the agreement they had reached at Mort Shmuni Church was no longer valid.

It was reported that Galle answered for the Protestants by saying that if this was the case, they would face their destiny alone without any help and without causing any problems for their Jacobite brothers. He offered forgiveness in advance but also warned Hanne that their turn to be in the crosshairs of the Muslim invaders was close at hand. Sadly, his prediction would be realized sooner rather than later.

A famous quotation from a prominent German citizen was made some thirty years after these events regarding the genocide that took place in the German concentration camps of World War II that sounds so much like the position that Hanne Safer adopted:

> *First, they came for the socialists, and I did not speak out—because I was not a socialist.*
>
> *Then they came for the trade unionists, and I did not speak out—because I was not a trade unionist.*
>
> *Then they came for the Jews, and I did not speak out—because I was not a Jew.*
>
> *Then they came for me—and there was no one left to speak for me.*
> —Martin Niemöller

Hanne chose not to stand (or speak out) for his Protestant brothers; soon there would be no one to speak out or to defend him.

Not long after the meeting between Hanne and Galle, the government sent an official to Midyat to announce that residents were required to turn over all arms and ammunition to the local authorities. They directed the local Syriac leaders to relay this message to their Protestant brothers who spoke the same language. Hanne Safer followed up by calling for an assembly at which they directed their fellow Christians to surrender their weapons.

In June, soldiers began house-to-house searches for hidden arms, and they arrested many of the Armenian and Assyrian males they found. The captured men were imprisoned and tortured while they awaited trial and whatever fate would fall on them. It is thought that Hanne Safar assisted in these arrests, but not long afterward the betrayed Orthodox leader would himself become one of the victims of the bloody massacre.

Galle had been told (along with so many others) that if he would just renounce his Christian faith and convert to Islam, his life would be spared. He refused, of course, and was consequently executed along with all the others. One of the Kurdish attackers saw that Galle had a beautiful ring on his finger, which he wanted for himself. When he couldn't remove it from the finger of the dead Galle, he took out his dagger and cut off Galle's finger to get the ring.

Despite his Christian faith, over one hundred years later the mayor's office in Midyat (which is run today by Kurdish Muslims) still displays the portrait of this most honorable man. An obituary for Galle calling him a Syriac patriot stresses his unselfish political activities:

> Galle Hermiz (1859–1915) was born in Midyat in Mesopotamia. He lived 56 years and died at the hands of the Young Turks.

Hermiz sacrificed his life for the sake of his people and fellow countrymen. He was known throughout the area as a great thinker. In Midyat he worked on the administrative council for 21 years and served as mayor for a period of eight years. His name became well known among his people in Anatolia, Aleppo, Beirut, and in the whole of Mesopotamia for defending the rights of his people and the poor in particular. He fought against all kinds of oppression. He was a generous man, and his house was open to all people, which earned him the appreciation of everyone.

Galle Hermiz

THE ULTIMATE SACRIFICE

In July approximately thirty-nine adult males of the Hermiz families who had been imprisoned were given the opportunity to save their lives by renouncing their faith in Christ and becoming Muslim. When they refused, they were placed in chains and marched two by two approximately two or three miles outside of the city. It was reported by the city's residents that they could be heard singing hymns all along the way as they walked toward what they knew was certain death. They were taken to the top of a mound, stripped of their clothing, gunned down, and thrown over the cliff. Their dead bodies were then thrown into a deep well. It is speculated that the Hermiz men were among the first to be killed in Midyat because of their influence in the Christian community and their wealth. They were suspected and accused of funding the resistance, including the purchase of guns and ammunition, although there was no evidence of such.

We visited this very site a few years ago, and walking to the top of that mound, we were struck by what we saw below us. To this day the land just below the mound that was soaked in blood in 1915 is still unfit for vegetation. The fig trees and grape vines in that field no longer bear fruit. Yet immediately across the road the vegetation is lush by comparison. The contrast over one hundred years later took our breath away. We suddenly felt that we were on holy ground, territory that had been soaked with the blood of martyrs. We stood in humble silence for a few moments and then we prayed aloud, praising God for His worthiness and for His grace, having given these men the courage and faithfulness to pay the ultimate price.

The mound in Midyat from where the martyrs were thrown

The well

5

The Massacre of Midyat

A HIDING PLACE

Thomas, when writing about the events of September 1915, began with this disclaimer: "Being so young, I naturally missed a lot of the details and there is much that I do not remember at all. However, I think I remember most of what came under my observation and with which I had to do, if for no other reason than the fact that for some years later, I never laid my head on a pillow at night but what I went through in memory the entire scene again."

The Christian community of Midyat received a tip from a friendly Turkish soldier that the Kurds were planning to attack their city and to eliminate, one way or another, the entire Christian population. Understandably, this report caused great anxiety and confusion. Many of them quickly fled to other towns, where they hoped to fare better. Others remained to defend themselves, their homes, and their city against the invaders. Those who did remain gathered in central points to meet the attack of the Kurds.

Tirzah (Thomas's mother) gathered her young children and assembled along with others in a large row of houses. The houses were separated only by common concrete walls, and they made holes in these walls so that people could go from one house to another without going outside. Here they gathered for safety, hoping to avoid the inevitable attack. One can only imagine the intensity of emotions, the fervent prayers, the conversations of mothers with their children, the inevitable tears, and the efforts to comfort the inconsolable.

We know from interviews with some of the older surviving children, cousins of Thomas, that the godly Christian mothers did their best to prepare their little ones for the impending massacre that was now certain to befall their city. One recalled his dear mother saying something like "We don't know what's going to happen, maybe today, maybe tomorrow, maybe next month... but they will come. You will most certainly be taken from me, and they will try to convert you to be Muslim. But let me tell you this: if you deny Christ and adhere to the Muslim faith, you may spare your life for a little while, but you will spend eternity in hell. If you refuse and instead take a stand for Christ, they may kill you. But remember this: after they kill you, it may take five or ten minutes for your body to succumb to death, but then you will be immediately transported into the presence of Jesus, where you will live forever!"

Knowing that permanent separation was inevitable, Tirzah gathered her four-year-old son to her breast and told him of his father in America. Thomas's memory of Emmanuel was limited at best; nevertheless, she secured a promise from him that he would one day seek the opportunity to be reunited with his father. Tirzah then lovingly clothed both of her children with several layers so they would be sufficiently cared for. The older people knew from experience that the Kurdish invaders would plunder, taking all the clothes and other goods for their own families, so at least this was one way of possibly saving some of their clothing.

THE ASSAULT—MARTYRDOM AND SEPARATION

Some have reported that the massacre took place over a period of days, perhaps even weeks. But for Thomas it was just one particular night that would forever change the trajectory of his young life. All night long Thomas, along with his mother and other family members, could hear the firing of guns and battle cries from both sides, for under the cover of darkness the Kurds made their attack. There was horrific fighting in the streets as some of the Christian men gathered what few weapons they had and bravely went out to fight for their families, as Nehemiah once directed: "Fight for your brothers, your sons, your daughters, your wives, and your homes" (Nehemiah 4:14).

There was no end to the cruelty. Babies had their heads dashed against stone walls, or they were bayonetted and waved above their murderers' heads for sport. Women were dragged by their hair through the streets. Blood flowed everywhere. Approximately 300 Assyrian men fought courageously. There were not enough rifles to go around; when one man was killed, another would take up his rifle and continue the fight. The Christians were greatly outnumbered and utterly defeated.

When morning came, Thomas found himself in a room with approximately seventy others, mostly women and children, and a few very young men. They were all trying to keep as still as possible, since they could hear the voices of the Kurds out in the courtyard. A little boy began crying for his mother and was immediately hushed, but not before his cries were heard by the Kurds outside. Within minutes the Kurdish raiders were banging on the door that led to the room where four-year-old Thomas was huddled with his three-year-old sister, Bessie; his mother, Tirzah; his maternal grandmother, Hana; and his fifteen-year-old Uncle Abraham.

When the door was forced opened by the Kurds, they immediately began searching the young men to see if any of them had guns or ammunition on them. Finding ammunition on Abraham, they took it from him and slapped his face. Before they took him away, he stooped down and placed a kiss on Thomas's cheek. Thomas never forgot that tender expression, being moved to tears when he would talk about it even decades later. The next time Thomas saw him, his Uncle Abraham was lying dead in a pool of his own blood with a knife plunged into his chest. We are left to assume that his dead body was later disposed of in the same manner that most others were destroyed—covered in kerosene and burned beyond recognition.

Years later Thomas recalled, "Mother and Grandmother were taken out into the open courtyard, leaving my sister and me in the hall for some time. When Mother and Grandmother came back into the hall, blood was streaming from the side of their necks over their dresses. It appeared that someone had just taken a knife and torn flesh from their necks, thus torturing them rather than killing them outright when they refused to renounce their faith in Christ." We'll never know if the intent was simply to torture them. It was reported that sometimes throats were slit for the barbaric purpose of inflicting a slow and painful death.

Tirzah, Hana, and the children then went back out into the courtyard. For a while they were alone, undoubtedly suffering intensely. Thomas heard them say that they would lie on the ground as if dead until they could make their escape. As these dear saints looked up at a frightened Thomas and Bessie, no doubt they prayed with intensity for the safety and protection of their little ones, knowing that soon they would be separated from them for the rest of their lives.

It wasn't long before a Kurd came out of one of the doors leading into the courtyard. Seeing the two small children standing together, he came and took Thomas by the wrist, led him out of the yard and into the street, leaving Bessie behind. Brother and sister would never again be in each other's presence, a grief that would follow Thomas for the rest of his life.

Sometimes children were killed along with the adults, but just as often the younger ones were mercifully allowed to live. Some would end up in nearby orphanages and others were adopted by Muslim couples, especially those who had no children. They believed it meritorious if they brought them up as Muslims; this would go on their account in heaven, they believed. It is thought that Bessie was also taken from her mother's side by a different Kurd, adopted, and raised by a Muslim family. Throughout the years stories have been circulated about what may have happened to her, but we have not been successful in validating those stories.

As Thomas was led out onto the street, he saw many bodies of men, women, even children scattered on the streets. The stench of death was present everywhere in the city. A major battle had taken place during the night, and it was impossible to move about without stepping over the dead. One of his cousins said that later that day he witnessed the awful scene of children being placed onto a pile of wood to which fire was set. He claimed that remarkably no child was heard to cry out in pain. Can there be any other explanation than that God intervened and quickly called these little ones to come unto Him?

In the meantime, once separated from their young children, Tirzah and Hana made a temporary short-lived escape. Upon being discovered, they were again offered the opportunity to save their lives. The Muslim soldiers noted Tirzah's youth and beauty and told her that if she would deny her faith, agree to become Muslim, and consent to marry one of them, they would spare both of the ladies' lives. They guaranteed them a life of ease and comfort. Without hesitation, they refused.

The women were then taken before the Turkish magistrate, where they were put on trial for the singular crime of refusing to renounce their faith in Christ. They were of course found guilty, taken out into the courtyard, stood up in front of a wall, and facing a firing squad of Turkish soldiers, shot down as common criminals, martyrs for their faith.

The story of Tirzah's faith and subsequent martyrdom has been shared with thousands of people over the last one hundred years. For those of us who are her direct descendants, we find her sacrifice something to be highly esteemed and at the same time deeply sobering. Our lives in twenty-first-century America are so comfortable and our Christianity so mainstream. We haven't had to experience our material goods being stripped from us, let alone being forced to watch as our children are forcefully removed from our care. We've not been physically tortured, nor have we had to face a firing squad.

The Islamic marauders who decimated Midyat and murdered Tirzah did so because as followers of Mohammed, they sincerely believed that their god, Allah, had commanded them to conquer the world by whatever forceful means necessary. In contrast, Jesus told His disciples that the world would know them by their love. He rebuked Peter for using his sword, and the apostle Paul said that Christ's followers would be recognized by qualities such as peace, kindness, and gentleness.

Tirzah was not without options. She most likely could have spared not only her own life but also those of her children and her mother as well. Once the conflict was over, she could have no doubt lived in relative safety and security. Others made that choice. But walking in the steps of her Savior, Tirzah's face was "set like a flint"; in her hour of testing, she did not hesitate or waver. Empowered by the Holy Spirit, she closed her eyes in Midyat—and opened them in the presence of the Almighty!

Emmanuel, Tirzah, and Thomas

6

Post-Massacre

DECEPTION REALIZED

Two weeks after the general massacre that left the Protestant community of Midyat decimated, the governor approached Hanne Safar and told him that some soldiers were to be placed at his house. Safar correctly interpreted this as a declaration of war, and he warned his family and the Orthodox community at large about the imminent danger. Days later, Hanne Safar was killed, together with seventeen members of his family. It is reported that he tried to defend himself with the ceremonial sword that had been awarded to him by the sultan, only to have it forcefully removed from his hands and then used to behead him.

By the time the Kurds and the Turks had finished their campaign, the demographics in southeast Turkey were very different. Records from the Paris Peace Conference of 1919 confirmed massive reductions in the Assyrian and

Armenian populations. The effort to eradicate Christianity from the region was felt not only in the Protestant and Catholic communities; even the patriarch of the indigenous Syriac Orthodox Church reported that over 25,000 of their people had also been killed for their faith. After the hostilities settled down, some of the Christians slowly returned to pick up their broken lives.

ADOPTED AS A MUSLIM

Focusing our attention back to young Thomas, when he and his Kurdish captor got to the outskirts of Midyat, they encountered what seemed to the lad like a small army camp. A Turkish soldier stopped them, and after what must have been a strong verbal confrontation, the soldier slapped the Kurd's face and took the boy from him. He then placed Thomas on a donkey and took him to a neighboring town. The naked bodies of the dead were strewn along the side of the road where they had been killed, a graphic and horrific sight, the memory of which would haunt young Thomas for years to come.

On the way to their intended destination, they spent one night in a friendly Kurd's home. It was here that Thomas was stripped of the extra clothes his mother had placed on him. He was left with only a single dress as the "extras" were stolen for the couple's children to wear. The first night of his separation from his mother and everyone and everything that he had ever known caused Thomas to cry all night long. Overwhelming fear and anxiety gripped the tender heart of this four-year-old little boy.

The next morning the soldier started out with Thomas for Astal, about eight to ten miles from Midyat. We will never know the soldier's intentions. Did he plan to take him for his own? Or perhaps he knew someone in Astal who might be interested in raising a little boy? Either way, in the providence of God, most likely unknown to the soldier, Thomas had an aunt who had settled in Astal with her Muslim husband. And on this day Aunt Medjida and her daughter, Miriam, "just happened" to be standing in the public square as the donkey bearing the soldier and Thomas entered the city.

Miriam took hold of her mother's hand and said to her, "Mommy, Mommy—there is Cousin Thomas with that soldier!" Medjida went to the soldier and begged him to let her have him. And he did. In God's amazing providence, the soldier had taken Thomas to the one place in this Muslim-dominated community where his aunt resided, and at just the very moment she had come into the public square.

We don't know many details of Aunt Medjida's story, but to his dying day Thomas held a special place in his heart for this dear aunt and for the important role she played in his young life. But unlike Tirzah, Medjida had chosen a different way forward. The thought of being forever separated from her children was more than she could bear, so when challenged, she denied the Christian faith in order to save her life, and although never actually converting to Islam, nevertheless had married a Muslim man, which was enough to prevent her from being tortured and the certain death that would follow.

For reasons not known to us, Medjida was unable to provide a home for Thomas herself, but she knew just the right couple in the same village with whom she could entrust her nephew, believing they would care for him well. Under Medjida's watchful eye, the Muslim couple took him in and began raising him as their own son. Darwish and Fatima Piskali were childless, and they joyfully welcomed the opportunity to adopt Thomas, showing him genuine love and affection.

Tirzah's brother Yusuf, who had somehow survived the conflict, was trying to rebuild his life in Midyat. Upon discovering that Aunt Medjida had placed Thomas with a Muslim family, he was not at all pleased with the arrangement. He arranged for Thomas to be brought to what was left of his home in Midyat, only to realize that things were still just too dangerous to live there. He then took Thomas with him to a neighboring city where he hoped to make a go of things.

However, they were very short of food, and one day Uncle Yusuf sent young Thomas out to beg for something to eat. Coming from a wealthy family and having been taught not to accept food from strangers made this an extremely difficult task. He was not a successful beggar, coming back to his uncle at the end of the day empty-handed.

Almost immediately after this experience, Thomas became deathly ill. It was reported that many people died during the long, cold winter following the massacre as typhoid and other diseases swept the area. Thomas's condition was never diagnosed, but there is some period following his begging expedition for which he had no recollection, most likely a period of unconsciousness.

Uncle Yusuf started rethinking his decision; he was afraid that his nephew might die due to his limited ability to properly care for him. He reached out to Medjida and told her that if her friends were in a better position to care for him, he would release him. So one day as Thomas was outside getting some needed sunlight, who should come into the courtyard but Fatima Piskali, riding on a donkey!

The Piskalis changed his name to "Jamiel" and taught him to speak Arabic as opposed to his native Assyrian tongue. They were anxious to bring him up in the Muslim faith and tradition. Thomas wrote many years later, "Under their kind and much-needed care, I naturally learned to love them, and, of course, their religion became mine. They instilled a prejudice in me against Christianity and all Christians. During my life with them, which lasted several years, whenever I saw any of my Christian relatives, I would shun them for fear they would take me."

During the approximately five years that Thomas lived in this home, he was taught the ways and habits of the Muslim faith. Remembering this indoctrination as an adult, he often referred to Islam as "the religion of hate." This was not based on something he read in a book but upon his lived experience. For the most part, the people of Astal were not as devoutly religious as one might expect. For example, to the best of his memory, most did not stop at the accustomed times to pray, a foundational tenet of the Muslim religion.

Fatima, on the other hand, was more religious than most and was usually faithful in keeping the daily prayer periods. She always fasted during the month of Ramadan. Despite her faithfulness to the rituals of prayer and fasting, when she socialized with the women in the neighborhood, Thomas remembered that "she would exchange some of the filthiest stories imaginable." This led the impressionable Thomas to perceive that the Islamic religion was not a religion of the heart. The transformation of heart and mind and the moral goodness that is expected of Christians (Romans 12:2) did not seem to him to have a corresponding effect in the religion of Islam.

Muslim boys in Astal learned the art of war early in life. Boys in each community would team up against boys in other communities and throw stones at each other with slings, such as perhaps David used when he killed Goliath. Every boy knew how to make a sling out of twine, and Thomas was no exception. More than once he went home with a head wound from one of these pretend wars, and he remembered that each time Fatima would get hysterical at the sight of his blood. But of course, she always lovingly bandaged his wounds and would then take him onto her lap and shower kisses on him.

Fatima was very kind to Thomas. Again, he wrote of her love for him: "I knew she loved me dearly and I thank God that during this time I was so well loved! I am sure that this love brought some healing to my mind and spirit. No one knows how much care and affection a child needs after passing through such traumatic experiences as I had been through."

THE RESCUE

Another very important person in Thomas's young life was his cousin Benjamin. At this point in the story (1919), Benjamin would have been in his late teens, while Thomas was just eight years old. For motivations that we don't quite understand, Benjamin volunteered for the Turkish army. A year later he went AWOL. Through mutual relatives, he became aware that Thomas was still alive and he couldn't bear the thought that his young cousin was not being raised by someone in the Hermiz family, such as possibly an aunt or an uncle who had survived the massacre.

Benjamin Hermiz

He also feared that "Tommy" (as he called him) was being indoctrinated into the religion of Islam. On top of those concerns, Benjamin knew that if Emmanuel, Tommy's father, was made aware that his son was still alive, he would most certainly wish to be reunited with him. He was determined to rescue Tommy from the Muslim family.

Claiming to be his uncle, Benjamin sought permission from the government to claim Tommy. In so doing, he put his own life at risk since as an AWOL soldier, he was not exactly on good terms with the government. Remarkably, he was awarded the necessary written permission for the purpose of retrieving his cousin.

Arriving in Astal, permit in hand, Benjamin was (not surprisingly) met with hostility by Darwish and Fatima. Initially Ben tried his diplomatic best to diffuse their disappointment and anger, reminding them that Tommy's natural father was living in America and was entitled to be reunited with his only son. He assured them that Emmanuel would compensate them for their services, and he expressed appreciation that they had nursed Tommy back to health and had lovingly cared for his emotional needs as well.

The Piskalis acknowledged that Ben might have an official document stating that he had a legal right to remove Tommy from their home, but Fatima especially was livid. Ben recalled that she pronounced curses on him. Among other harsh words she said, "I hope you go blind and have your neck broken!" Undeterred, Ben hoisted his cousin onto his back, but Tommy started crying, kicking, and screaming. Ben soon became exhausted and frustrated with all the crying and resistance, so he put him down, pulled out his gun, and put it in Tommy's back. (Apparently that's what you call taking charge of the situation!) In the moment, at least, Benjamin won the day—and they were off!

A day and a half later the boys arrived in Mardin, where Benjamin left his cousin in the care of the Congregational missionaries at the orphanage. Two of Ben's younger sisters and his brother were already living there because their mother had died shortly after the massacre and their father, Jacob, was one of the three brothers who had fled years earlier to America. The plan was for Tommy to remain in the care of the missionaries until arrangements could be made for his travel to the United States. Of course, this would prove to be an extremely difficult assignment. The first hurdle was Tommy's own resistance.

After Tommy's first night in the orphanage, Ben went the following morning to visit with his siblings and cousins—and was immediately informed by one of his sisters that Tommy was gone! An older "uncle" from his Muslim family had come on horseback and taken him back to Astal to be with his adoptive family. Ben took off after the man, who was not about to let Ben take him again regardless of whatever official papers he could produce. When Ben caught up with them, the Muslim man said, "Listen—I'm warning you once and for all. This boy belongs to us. If you bother us again, I will put a bullet in your head; I will kill you like a dog!"

At this point Ben realized the "fight" was going to require more than he could accomplish on his own. In February 1920 he emigrated to the United States, where he would settle with his father, Jacob, in Rhode Island. But first he had a mission: to meet face to face with Uncle Emmanuel, who after receiving an honorable discharge after the war, had once again settled in Pittsburgh. Ben quickly brought him up to date on activities in Turkey and most importantly, the news that his son Thomas was alive. Emmanuel the warrior went into action!

7

Bound for America

EMMANUEL'S EFFORTS

Emmanuel was overjoyed to know that his son was alive and well. Being a man of action, he was determined to do whatever was necessary to bring Thomas to America. But there was one huge stumbling block: the Turkish government was not permitting male children to leave the country. If father and son were going to be reunited, it would require some initiative and intervention from the American side of things, and possibly some subversive action to get around the Turkish government's mandate.

Emmanuel was beyond frustrated when he heard Benjamin's story of the attempted rescue and subsequent failure to keep Thomas at the orphanage. The more he thought about it, the angrier he became. He desperately needed to find a way to get Thomas away from the Muslim family, back into the orphanage, and ultimately on a ship destined for America. On advice from a friend, he decided to pay a visit to the Pittsburgh chapter of the American Red Cross. But how would he provoke someone's focused attention? How would he effectively translate his own sense of urgency in such a way as to inspire someone else to take action?

According to Benjamin's accounting of the story, the meeting with the Red Cross went something like this:

> Emmanuel was mad. And he was still sick because of inhaling the poisonous gas in the battlefields of southern France. He bundled up his army uniform, his medals, his army-issued coat, even his gas mask, and stormed into the office of the American Red Cross. As the young lady behind the counter saw him approaching, she braced herself for what was coming. Emmanuel threw the bundle on the counter to make sure he had her full attention. And then in his best broken English he said, "I'm mad! You know I volunteered to fight for Uncle Sam. I fought, and here I am—no longer a real man 'cause I was gassed. I got one boy in the old country. If Uncle Sammy can't help me get him to the USA, Uncle Sammy can take this coat, this uniform, and these medals, and you know what you can do with them!"

A LEGACY OF FORGIVENESS

We don't know her name, but we thank God for placing this special woman in that office on that day. There must have been something in Emmanuel's voice, something in his eyes, that resonated in her spirit. Her compassion for this suffering veteran drove her to action. She wanted to know the full story and promised to help Emmanuel get his boy to America. She assured him that Uncle Sam had the power to work behind the scenes, and if necessary, to even smuggle the young boy out of the country. Emmanuel gave her all the information she asked for, and she promptly sent an urgent request to Washington, DC.

We'll never know all the many details that followed in the weeks ahead, but clearly, there were many letters, phone calls, and perhaps other forms of communication between the Pittsburgh chapter of the Red Cross, government officials in Washington, the American Missionary Society, and friendly organizations in the Middle East. We know that a small ransom was paid and that additional funds were supplied to cover Thomas's eventual travel expenses. There was no American consulate in Midyat or Astal, of course, so communications were directed to the consulate in Aleppo, Syria, which in turn arranged for the logistics of such a mission. Instructions included firing off a cable to Agnes Fenenga at the orphanage in Mardin. Miss Fenenga was directed to get Tommy Hermiz (aka Jamil) in Astal at such-and-such house. She was provided with a soldier for protection, and together they made the two-day horseback ride, going directly to the Piskalis' house.

Miss Fenenga spotted Tommy in the kitchen and pointed him out to the soldier. Fatima protested, saying "This is my boy!" The sweet but determined Miss Fenenga responded with equal boldness, "This is not your boy—he is our boy. His father is in America, and he has demanded to be reunited with his only son." The soldier proceeded to put him onto his horse as Fatima cried out in agony and Tommy wept. It was a bitter farewell; they literally had to drag him away from the woman he had come to accept and love as his mother. As they traveled again toward Mardin, Tommy continued crying and wailing until finally the soldier could no longer stand it. He slapped him across the face to make him stop crying. The remainder of the journey was very quiet.

LIVING IN THE ORPHANAGE

This time it would not be so easy for Tommy to escape from the school; he wasn't given as much liberty to roam around as he had been given before. Practically all the children in the school were those belonging to martyred Christian parents; it had effectively become an orphanage. Among the other children there, Tommy had four female cousins and two male cousins, all of whom belonged to his uncles Jacob and Alexander, now living in the United States. Some of the children were blessed to have fathers living in the United States who would eventually make provision for them to come to America.

Most of us will never be able to fully understand what these precious little children went through. Even attempting to think about their pain is heartbreaking. At least one of Tommy's cousins didn't make it. Even after rejoining her father in the US, she became entirely unbalanced from the shock of all she had witnessed, and she never recovered. Miss Fenenga and the other missionaries did an amazing job of caring for them until they could be reunited with their fathers. Most of them were able to overcome their trauma and lead fully productive lives in America, some of them even excelling in their chosen fields of endeavor.

Approximately two months after Tommy was taken from their home, the Piskalis tried again to remove Tommy from the orphanage and return him to their home. But the missionaries stood their ground and refused to release him. Remember: they were on solid legal grounds based on the official papers that Benjamin had previously secured from the Turkish government.

And something else had changed. By this time, Tommy had been under the strong influence of the Christians in the school, especially an older cousin by the name of Yusuf, who had a wonderful impact in his life, teaching him how to pray and memorize scripture. Slowly but surely, Tommy was being weaned away from the Muslim faith to again embrace Christianity as his religion. Not that he understood much about either one at this young age, and not that he had become a true believer, but it was enough to sufficiently satisfy him that he might be better off to reconnect with his original family and their religion. He had begun looking forward with anticipation to making the long journey to America, where he could once again be with his father, a man he barely remembered.

THE ESCAPE

Thomas remained in this school for approximately a year, waiting for arrangements to be completed for his secret departure from the country. Obviously this type of operation takes time and careful planning, but the American Red Cross and their partners came through. When the time was right, Tommy was placed on a cattle boat (that's right—a cattle boat) traveling south on the Euphrates River, destined for Aleppo in northern Syria, and was effectively smuggled out of his homeland.

The next step was an uncomfortable, no-frills train ride to Beirut, Lebanon, followed by a delay of several months awaiting a proper passport. Although the many specific details of this timeframe are unknown to us, we do know that he was being protected under the supervision of the Red Cross and that his needs were being cared for by an unnamed American missionary. Eventually he was placed in the company of an Armenian family who was also emigrating to the United States.

In those days it would have taken several weeks to travel between Beirut and New York City. They first traveled across the Mediterranean to Marseilles in southern France. Then it was another train ride to northern France, making several overnight stops, and finally boarding an Italian ship at a northern port and sailing across the Atlantic to New York City.

The ship arrived in New York sometime shortly after Christmas Day 1920. The process went something like this: Before the ship was allowed to enter New York Harbor, it had to stop at a quarantine checkpoint off Staten Island, where doctors boarded the ship and set about to look for dangerous and contagious diseases such as smallpox, yellow fever, plague, cholera, and leprosy; at the time, this was about a three-day process. Once the ship passed inspection, passengers were allowed to disembark onto Ellis Island.

FATHER-AND-SON REUNION

On Ellis Island were large halls for sleeping quarters, one for men and one for women. That first night Thomas slept in one of those large halls with what seemed to him to be about two hundred men and boys, all sleeping on double- and triple-deck bunk beds. He remembered sleeping on a lower bunk. Morning came too soon for him, and when the awakening bell rang, he opened his eyes but decided to get a little more sleep.

When he finally awakened, he found himself all alone in this large hall and in semi-darkness. Understandably, he was frightened. He found his way to a large double door and began pounding on it, crying all the while. Some men opened the door and, seeing him crying, they comforted him, took him to the dining room, and gave him a good breakfast. Then they filled his pockets with some English walnuts. No one scolded him for oversleeping. This treatment made quite an impression on the nine-year-old; this was his first taste of what he would later term "American gentility and kindness."

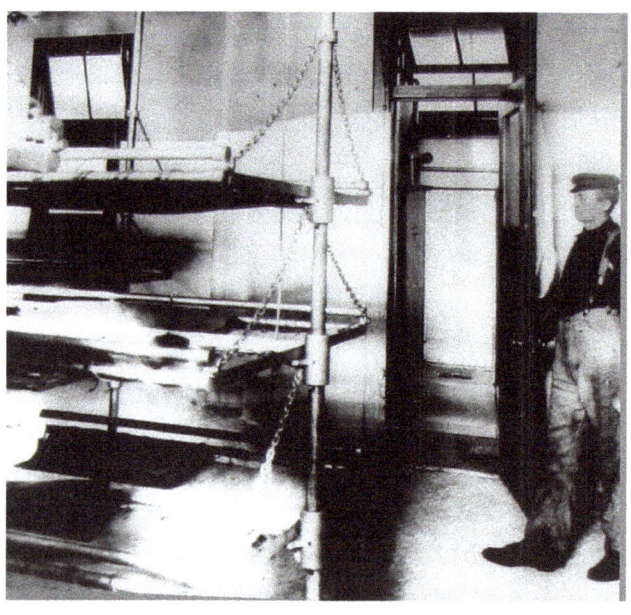

Sleeping quarters on Ellis Island where Thomas slept

Once Thomas was released from quarantine, Emmanuel was informed and quickly made his way to New York on New Year's Day 1921. Keep in mind that father and son had been separated now for several years; Emmanuel didn't have any idea what his nine-year-old son looked like! And the same was true for Thomas of his father. Quite a few names of immigrants were announced to appear that morning before the customs officials to be processed. Thomas's name was called, as well as those of the Armenian family with whom he was traveling. They were taken into a room with about fifty other people. As they went into this room, a tall soldier in a khaki uniform stood in the doorway watching the proceedings. Thomas sat near the middle of the room next to the aisle, waiting to be processed. As he sat there he played with a handkerchief, which dropped onto the floor. And as it did, the tall soldier came over, bent down, picked it up, and handed it to him.

Moments later Thomas was called to the front of the room for processing. As he was giving his name to the officials, the same soldier came striding down the aisle and started talking to the customs people in English, a language unknown to Thomas. Finally he turned, knelt down, and looked directly into the eyes of this scared little boy, and now speaking in Arabic, said, "Do you know who I am?" Thomas had no idea. Emmanuel then introduced himself, informed him that he was his father, and embraced him. It was an amazing moment in which Thomas hardly knew how to respond. After all the suffering he had been through—he was now safe in his father's arms!

A LEGACY OF FORGIVENESS

Thomas, 1921

Emmanuel with son Thomas from the *Pittsburgh Post*, February 6, 1921

8

Becoming Americanized

1921-1926

Before settling together in Pittsburgh, Emmanuel took Thomas to visit with his uncles Jacob and Alexander in Rhode Island. These men were previously unknown to Thomas as they had left Turkey when Thomas was only one year old. No doubt it was healthy for Thomas to spend some time bonding with his uncles. On the way back to Pittsburgh, Emmanuel taught his son his first English words, including "thank you." A visit to the Red Cross office was Emmanuel's next priority so that he and Thomas could show proper appreciation to those who had made this reunion possible.

In October of that year, 1921, Emmanuel received a letter from one of his brothers who was still living in Midyat. Due to the authoritarian restrictions of the Turkish government, this piece of mail had to be smuggled out of the country to guarantee that it would arrive at its destination without first being opened. A friendly British officer had hand-carried the letter to where it could be safely mailed to America. Emmanuel's brother had some startling news for him.

Could there possibly be another reunion on the horizon? The whereabouts of Bessie, Thomas's kid sister, had been unknown since the day of the assault on Midyat. Emmanuel's brother said that he had seen Bessie with his own eyes, that she was being held in a Kurdish camp of some kind. He had approached them, requested to meet with Bessie, and was promptly turned away on threat that if he made any attempt to remove Bessie, both she and he would be killed. Emmanuel and Thomas were overcome with hope.

Prior to receiving this information, Emmanuel had assumed that Bessie had been murdered. Thomas, on the other hand, had been holding onto the hope that his sister had been treated in much the same fashion as he had been, that she was hopefully alive and being cared for by a good family. Once again Emmanuel went to the American Red Cross to see what they could do. Unfortunately, their efforts never accomplished the desired results. Bessie's life story remains a mystery to this day. We have heard stories about what may have happened to her but unfortunately have never been able to validate with any certainty how her life may have unfolded.

Life for father and son in Pittsburgh got off to a rough start. Emmanuel certainly loved his son, but he didn't exactly have a nurturing personality. Emmanuel was a warrior, not a caregiver. Single-parenting a ten-year-old boy was simply, as we say in our modern vernacular, "not in his wheelhouse." Emmanuel was having his own physical problems due to the chemicals that were still in his system from the war. He would sometimes pass out, fall on the sidewalk, and later be picked up by the police for drunkenness, which was not the case. A doctor advised him that he should consider working in a steel mill, where he might eventually sweat the chemicals out of his system, a suggestion with which he complied..

And . . . Thomas was a handful. He could barely speak a full sentence in English, which contributed to communication issues at home, but even worse problems at Hancock Public School. We all know how cruel kids can be to each other, and when Thomas would open his mouth to speak at school, he was quickly laughed at and bullied. Like his father, Thomas was not afraid to stand his ground, and he continually came home from school bearing the bruises and bloodstains that followed from getting into fist fights. This added to Emmanuel's frustration.

Once again Emmanuel consulted with the Red Cross, and this time they came through, finding a boarding home in which Thomas could live. For the next two years Thomas would be well cared for in the home of a large Christian family who would not only help him with his English, but more importantly, teach him solid Christian principles and the best parts of American culture. By the end of his first year in their home, he had all but forgotten Arabic and was speaking English fluently. But although they taught him well and took him to church and Sunday School, he continued displaying serious anger issues, which often got him in trouble. The circumstances of his childhood had deposited a bitterness deep in his soul that prevented a sense of well-being, and that threatened to destroy any hope of a good future.

Unfortunately, it became necessary for his host family to relocate to Cleveland, and twelve-year-old Thomas was back sharing a room with his father. The next three years were very unstable. He would spend a few months with his father, then go to Rhode Island to live with his uncles for a while, then back to Pittsburgh for a period. Bouncing back and forth so much made it next to impossible to settle into any kind of solid family life.

With tears in his eyes, Thomas said he would always remember his uncle, bidding him farewell the last time he made the move from Rhode Island to Pennsylvania. Years later, Uncle Jacob told Thomas what had been on his mind, that he had lost all hope of Thomas's ever amounting to anything. He fully expected that he would eventually, in his words, "go to the dogs," most likely spending his adult life in prison. This painful expectation grieved Jacob's soul, but his concerns were probably well founded.

Among his adolescent vices, Thomas had become addicted to the pleasure of watching movies. While traveling to America from Turkey, the time he spent in France had opened the world of motion pictures to his nine-year-old eyes. On the surface this sounds harmless enough, even tame to our modern ears. One might think that in his state of brokenness, it would have been understandable and acceptable for him to allow his mind and emotions to get lost in the world of entertainment. But he would come to see this period of his life as a moral wasteland. He went so far as to say that being so totally enraptured by the medium was, he believed, psychologically damaging. Instead of applying himself in school or engaging in sports or other wholesome and healthy pursuits, he allowed his mind to become obsessed with fantasy. The only thing that kept him from spending more time at the movie theater was his lack of money.

Undoubtedly there were other sins committed during his teenage years, of which Thomas chose not to speak or write. But suffice it to say that the trajectory of his life was self-destructive. He was foul-mouthed, hot-tempered, rebellious, and anti-social. It was hard to see how this young man was going to be able to make anything out of his life. Perhaps the trauma of those early years was just too much to overcome. At age fifteen he dropped out of school altogether, lied about his age, and started working in the local foundry where his father was employed. An explosion in the plant nearly took his life, but God had other plans.

THE ROAD TO CONVERSION

Thomas did start becoming aware of a growing desire in his heart to, in his words, "be good." But he discovered that his strong will was not strong enough; he couldn't muster enough willpower to reform himself. His constant failings got the best of him, and he couldn't see any "good" way forward. In his words, "I did not yet understand the power of the gospel and what Christ could do for me."

God's providential mercy was evident when Thomas and Emmanuel moved once again, this time next door to a family who attended a small Primitive Methodist Church in the area. The mother would often invite Thomas to their Sunday School, but he would always come up with an excuse for not going with them. Finally, after tenaciously being invited again and again, perhaps just to get her off his back, he consented to go.

There was a huge stumbling block in the way of Thomas's embracing religion of any kind. He had been exposed to the followers of Mohammed, and he wasn't terribly impressed. It seemed to him that of the ones he knew, most were not particularly happy and that although they had a lot of rules with which they were supposed to comply, most of them didn't. Based on his early life's experiences, theirs was an obviously violent religion, which made no sense to him. He had also known a fair number of nominal Christians whose lives didn't seem to offer much of a contrast to their Muslim counterparts. There were marvelous exceptions to this of course, but he was generally wary of anyone who claimed to have religion.

So when Thomas was introduced to David Hood as his Sunday School teacher, he was certainly skeptical. But there was something different about this man—he seemed to enjoy his religion! That was a new thing, to see someone happy in his faith. When thinking back on it, Thomas wrote that "His face shone with the joy of the Lord!" He thought, *How fortunate to have a religion like that!* This should be a good reminder for all of us that we should never reduce Christianity to a matter of demands, resolutions, and willpower; "The joy of the Lord is our strength," and in this case it was by far the best witness. That's what Thomas saw in Mr. Hood. He didn't understand it, but he definitely longed for it.

Another example of religious skepticism and confusion in Thomas's young mind was regarding the afterlife. Muslims and Christians alike spoke of heaven. Thomas figured that if anyone was good enough and did enough good works, he or she would probably get to go there. Maybe Mr. Hood's joy was due in part to his understanding that he didn't have to prove to God that he was somehow worthy of heaven but that in fact, his welcome into heaven was based on Christ's worthiness and His sacrifice on our behalf. There were so many things he didn't understand about Christianity, but something kept him listening.

After listening repeatedly to his pastor, his Sunday School teacher, and a visiting evangelist, he knew he needed what they were talking about, but he was still unsure about how to appropriate such a faith. He tried turning over a new leaf, even going forward in response to old-fashioned altar calls a couple of times, but that always failed to make a difference. Finally one morning before leaving for work, he knelt beside his bed and poured out his heart to the Lord. For the first time, he acknowledged that he was lost, that he had come to understand he was a sinner incapable of fixing himself, and that Christ had died to be his Savior. Here is the way Thomas described the event that forever changed his life:

> God, in His abundant wisdom and mercy, looked down deep in my heart, and He must have seen a real desire in me to be a Christian. In His love and tender mercy, He came to my heart that morning. I arose from my knees a new creature, though I couldn't have explained to anyone what had happened to me, for I didn't understand it myself. But from then on my life was completely changed. I went back to the foundry and found that I did not have to curse and swear. There was a new power in my life that put me above this low living. I began going to prayer meetings, where I heard Christians testify to being "saved." I began to understand that this was exactly what had happened to me and soon joined them in this testimony. It was a reality! Life was now different!

The transformation in Thomas's life was significant, and he was anxious to share with others the joy he now experienced, including his father. We hold in our possession a letter dated September 28, 1928. Emmanuel was writing to a relative still living in Midyat at that time. We cherish the portion where he writes, "I stay with Thomas in the same room. Thomas is very, very good. I am working in a steel mill and Thomas is thinking about being a pastor. Thomas says I must give my life to Jesus" (see appendix B).

SANCTIFICATION

Approximately one year later, Thomas had another experience as a result of attending "Everybody's Mission," where he was exposed to the Wesleyan teaching of entire sanctification. Here are his own words that describe what he and those of like doctrine refer to as the "second work of grace"—

> I had quit working at the foundry and was now working in a wholesale drug house in Pittsburgh. I formed the habit of reading the Bible on my knees before going to work. About this time I was reading in the Psalms. This particular morning I was reading Psalm 32. When I came to the eighth verse something happened to me, for it said, "I will instruct thee and teach thee in the way which thou shalt go: I will guide thee with mine eye" [KJV]. It was all I needed. Something within me gave way completely to the will of God. I have never had a controversy with God since then. There was a difference in my life as the Spirit of God seemed to take a new control of my will and affections. God

filled me with His Spirit that day. Even those at work seemed to sense something different about me, though they had known me as a born-again Christian for about a year. I seemed to have gained poise as a result of this experience.

Perhaps the reason that Thomas was so moved as he read Psalm 32 that morning was that he had been struggling spiritually with a door that had closed to him. He had been sensing for a while that God wanted him to preach and so was anxious to go to a school where he could study the Bible in depth. He applied to attend the Christian and Missionary Alliance's Bible school at Nyack, New York, on the Hudson River but was rejected because he did not have a high school diploma. He later described the reaction of his heart as "somewhat rebellious," an attitude he knew wasn't right.

When he prayed over the reading of Psalm 32 that morning, something within him gave way completely to the will of God. And what a sweet surrender it was! Reminiscent of Grandfather Thoma, he loved God and he loved God's Word! And so he surrendered to this temporary disappointment but would not give up on the idea of pursuing some formal Bible training with the expectation that the Lord would yet open doors of opportunity, both for study and for proclaiming the full counsel of God's holy Word.

9

Becoming a Servant of the Lord

RESPONDING TO THE CALL TO PREACH

Thomas continued growing spiritually, becoming firmly established in his Christian experience. Others took note of his maturing faith and his desire to proclaim the Good News. He did some street evangelism, preaching as loudly as he could so that passersby would get the message! Soon doors were opening for him to speak at youth meetings, prayer meetings, missions meetings, and more.

The board overseeing Everybody's Mission happened to be in session one day in an upstairs room at mission headquarters on Chatham Street. From the porch on the first level, Thomas was exhorting anyone who would listen, preaching salvation as they walked by. Apparently the board members approved of what they heard from their upstairs window—as they promptly decided to award

Thomas with a license to preach! A year later they formally ordained him for the ministry.

It was through his association with Everybody's Mission that he became acquainted with God's Bible School (GBS) in Cincinnati. In the spring of 1930, GBS accepted Thomas's application to attend as a "work student," giving him the opportunity to work his way through the school. Thomas was thrilled. The only "catch" was that at some point he would need to attend and graduate from high school before he could take some of the more advanced classes.

For the first two years his studies were focused on the Bible, church history, missions, and related topics. In year three, still residing at GBS, he added several high school courses to his curriculum. The following year, he left GBS, moved to Lancaster, Ohio, and enrolled in a local high school. By doubling up on his course work, he graduated from high school in just two years. We

Thomas Hermiz
"A diligent student whose quiet determination will certainly, some day, spell unusual success for him."

—From the 1935 *Mirage*, Lancaster (Ohio) High School yearbook recently discovered that Thomas made the honor roll, something he had never shared with his family.

Unfortunately, Thomas was not able to return to GBS to complete his Bible studies, mostly for financial reasons. But in the decades that followed, we can say unequivocally that what he lacked in formal training, he more than made up for in private study. He was a voracious reader, amassing an enormous library, and was more importantly a perpetual learner at the feet of Jesus.

In 1933 he accepted the call to pastor a small mission church in Lancaster. This would begin his more than sixty years of pastoral ministry and his association with the Churches of Christ in Christian Union. While he was still living in Lancaster, another very important thing happened.

After a year of pastoring, Thomas began accepting opportunities to speak in weekend meetings, presenting not only the gospel message but also the unique story of his young life, including the inspirational story of his mother's martyrdom. On one such occasion in the fall of 1934, he was invited to preach for a weekend meeting at the denomination's church in Delaware, Ohio. The pastor had some additional duties that weekend, including dedicating a new mission church in Marysville, Ohio, roughly sixteen miles away.

The pastor invited Thomas to join him. He also asked him to drive his car and asked if he would be so kind as to give a ride to the Delaware church pianist. Her name was Violet Harris, and she was also the youth president. We're not sure how long it would have taken for him to drive that old Star sixteen miles with 1930s road conditions, but apparently it was just long enough for the couple to get acquainted, and Thomas was quite taken with her. The following Memorial Day weekend (1935), in front of a packed auditorium at the Delaware church, and exactly one day after Thomas received his long-awaited high school diploma, Violet Harris became Mrs. Violet Hermiz.

Rev. & Mrs. Thomas E. Hermiz, May 30, 1935

PASTORING AND RAISING A FAMILY

And just who was this fair maiden who so captivated Thomas's heart? Her background could not have been more different from his. Violet was the oldest of nine children, and by all accounts, hers was a very happy and stable childhood. Guy and Bessie Harris raised a very close family on Delaware's Eaton Street. The local church was the center of their activities, and several of the siblings would go on to serve the Lord in fulltime Christian service.

A musical and creative bunch they were. Many evenings they would gather around the piano and sing the great hymns of the faith or maybe just listen to Guy's original folksy compositions played on the guitar. And the children would act out the plays they had written during the day to entertain themselves. So yes, the fair-skinned, sheltered, protected, happy, and contented homebody who was Violet was very different from the more serious, olive-complected, traumatized young man who had rarely and only briefly tasted of stability in the numerous places he had lived. Yet somehow she was perfect for him. Never underestimate what God can do for two young people who share a love for Christ and have surrendered their lives to Him.

Over the next sixty-plus years, Thomas pastored several churches in five states, and he and Violet raised a family of six children: three boys and three girls. The first pastorate following their wedding was a little country church in Urbana, Ohio. After one year, Thomas was called to pastor the church in Delaware where they had been married, Violet's home church.

These were Depression years and these small churches had very little money with which to pay a pastor's salary. Thomas was paid $10 per Sunday—every other Sunday. (He obviously didn't go into ministry for the money!) He did take special meetings, usually held in tents, and mostly in the summer, which among the more important spiritual motivations, did help a bit with the finances, which in turn helped support their expanding family. Both of their first two children (Teresa and Tom) were born at home while they lived and pastored in Delaware from 1936 to 1939.

TRAGEDY STRIKES AGAIN

Throughout the summer of 1938, Thomas had been feeling a somewhat unique and overwhelming burden for his father, so much so that he had asked the church to be in prayer for Emmanuel's salvation. Several weeks of intense intercession passed, and a few of the folks, including Thomas, were starting to sense some release from the burden, and hope of a breakthrough was rising in Thomas's heart. He knew God had heard the cry of his heart. Could Emmanuel's long-awaited salvation be imminent?

On August 13 at approximately 11:00 p.m. the phone rang. The voice on the other end of the phone informed Thomas that his father had been shot. The men had been drinking together at a neighborhood bar, and an argument ensued over something insignificant. As things started heating up and moving toward a physical altercation, the men were separated and each of them began walking toward his own house. According to what was reported, after thinking about it, Emmanuel felt bad about the situation and decided to go directly to the other man's house to make peace with him. It was not to be.

When the man observed Emmanuel coming toward his house, he wrongly interpreted his actions and quickly grabbed his revolver. Once Emmanuel reached within twenty-five feet of his house, the man opened his door and without exchanging words shot him point blank. Emmanuel was unarmed. An ambulance was summoned, but somewhere between the point of this crime and the hospital, Emmanuel breathed his last breath. Once again, violence had touched the Hermiz family. Charges were never filed, and a brokenhearted Thomas went on with his life, harboring no ill will toward the one who had killed his father.

Let that sink in for just a minute. The culture in which the Hermiz family had existed for generations was one of retribution and vengeance. Surely Emmanuel's life was thus defined. He lived (and died) "by the sword." And years earlier, it had looked as if Thomas was destined for a similar lifestyle. But Thomas, who had long since forgiven the Muslims who had robbed him of his mother, now by the grace of God forgave the man who had taken his father's life. In so doing, the power of that generational sin was broken!

EXPANDED FAMILY AND EXPANDED MINISTRY

In the spring of 1939 Thomas was invited to tell his life story and conduct a revival meeting in Athens, Pennsylvania. He was well received, which resulted in his being invited to pastor the local church. After much prayer, Thomas and Violet were united in sensing that God was calling them to go there. This was the beginning of twenty-five years of fruitful ministry in both Pennsylvania and upstate New York. In addition to pastoring and church planting throughout the region, Thomas served several years as a district superintendent. During his pastoring years in Pennsylvania, three more children were added to the family—Joseph, Ruthie, and Mary Esther. Their sixth and final addition, John, was born during Thomas's pastorate in Endicott, New York.

While Violet tended to the needs at home, she also supported her husband in ways that cannot be measured in human terms; her life was absolutely defined by the time she spent on her knees, as a true prayer warrior. She was also an amazing if uncomfortable hostess, opening the parsonage to countless missionaries and traveling evangelists. She facilitated the strong missions focus in their home, hosting prayer meetings and keeping in contact with many pioneer missionaries all over the world. This shared focus with her husband encouraged him to take a lead role in the World Gospel Mission's New York state activities.

Thomas thoroughly enjoyed these years of ministering in the Northeast. Those who sat under his public ministry observed some things about him—he had the heart of a pastor-shepherd, the mind of an apologist, and the fearlessness of a missionary. Those who encountered him "off the platform" knew that he was an eternal optimist who always chose to believe the best about everyone he met. He was a well-read, self-educated student not only of the Bible but also of many other subjects. Civil debate was a skill he often displayed . . . uncompromising in his personal understanding of God's truth yet always seeking common ground with those of like faith. Back when the word *tolerance* meant something good, he was without equal among peers.

For those of us in the conservative and evangelical camp, the word *ecumenical* has a well-deserved negative connotation in our minds. But in the 1950s and 1960s, Thomas was an energetic participant in any genuine attempts at unity among the faithful. His attitude was one of great enthusiasm when there were opportunities to fellowship and to serve alongside those of other denominations. He would not at all be a fan of what this compromised movement has become today, but he took very seriously the apostle Paul's call for unity among the brethren.

10

Travels to the "Old Country"

SEARCHING FOR SISTER

In 1957 while living and pastoring a church in Endwell, New York, Thomas made the first of what would be several trips to the Middle East. This first trip was motivated by his longstanding desire to learn what he could about his sister's whereabouts and to potentially even find and reunite with Bessie. Leaving his congregation in the hands of his oldest son, Tom, he took the entire summer to, among other things, visit relatives in Lebanon and Syria. Unfortunately, although he relished the time to connect with those family members, most of whom he had never previously met, his attempts to visit Midyat and to find his sister were to no avail. At the time, Midyat was part of a military zone—and without a special authorization from the Turkish government, he was not permitted to visit there.

He spent some of this time touring Europe and several Middle Eastern countries, but by far the highlight of his journey was the time he spent in the Holy Land. The country of Israel was only nine years old at the time, and once he had the experience of "walking where Jesus walked," he was hooked and determined to return. He often spoke of the concluding moments of this tour, sailing into New York Harbor, as he had done thirty-six years earlier as a frightened nine-year-old boy. When the Statue of Liberty came into view, this first-generation immigrant became overwhelmed with emotion. He wept with deep feelings of gratitude to God that he had been blessed to be able to call America his adopted homeland.

THE FINAL JOURNEY

Over the next thirty-five years Thomas made several more trips to the "old country," as he called it, typically hosting tour groups to Israel, a place he had studied extensively and loved very much. Skipping ahead to March 1992, he made what would be his last trip, and this time he finally reached his childhood home of Midyat. Violet was able to accompany him for this memorable visit. Just before making the journey, in a letter to his daughter Mary Esther, then a missionary to Kenya, he stated that his primary goal for making the trip, for which he requested her prayers: to reopen and preach in the church his family had helped to found and where they worshiped in 1915. God would honor those prayers and fulfill his dream.

Thomas and Violet were guests of the archbishop of the Mor Gabriel Monastery, just fifteen miles from Midyat. Although we actually have no idea of what Thomas discussed with the archbishop when they met together, we have to believe that they would have engaged in conversation on matters of faith, perhaps essential beliefs they shared in common, and no doubt doctrines and practices they could not agree upon. But knowing Thomas, we feel it would have been a respectful conversation spoken with gentleness and full of grace.

Timotheos Samuel Aktaş, archbishop of the Mor Gabriel Monastery

The archbishop made arrangements for them to visit the old Protestant church, sending a couple of his assistants to accompany them as they toured the vacant church building where Thomas attended with his family when he was four years old. Additionally, the archbishop's people assisted them as they walked the streets of Thomas's childhood hometown. At one point along the way they stopped in front of one of the very large residences that belonged to the Hermiz family before the massacre. A nun who was walking with them recorded in her journal that as Thomas stood before his childhood home, his mind was flooded with memories and his heart overflowed with a variety of emotions, which he struggled to verbalize. Once again the tears flowed. The long-since-abandoned structure was a sight for his eyes to behold.

Thomas at his house in 1992   Thomas's house, restored 2012

There is another large mansion that was owned by the Hermiz family, this one built by Thoma's brother (Malky), which has seen some interesting history within its walls. Built in the late 1800s, it was truly a masterpiece, a large and magnificent piece of architecture (see appendix

C). Following the 1915 massacre, the Turks took control of this house and turned it into a regional military headquarters from 1915 until 1930. Based on what we have been told, this was most likely the very place where Tirzah and her mother faced their trial and the final moments of their earthly lives, the courtyard of which was where their bodies succumbed to the blast of bullets from the Turkish firing squad.

Fast-forward to the 21st century, and the mansion was acquired by a developer from Istanbul who in 2002 set about its restoration to, in his words, "keep a high fidelity to its original form." In 2011 the completely remodeled structure was opened to the public as a five-star luxury hotel called "Shmayaa."

Shmayaa Hotel, 2012; John, Mary Esther, Ruthie, Daniel

Having spent three nights there in 2012 with my sisters and my son, we can attest to its opulence. The poignancy of the moment did not escape us as we dined in the courtyard where ninety-seven years earlier, our grandmother gave her life's blood rather than deny her love for Christ.

Getting back to Thomas's long-awaited visit to Midyat, two more events highlighted this experience. The first took place at the Protestant church building known as Bethel. Thinking back to the genesis of this structure, grandfather Thoma had only dreamed about such a location for the gathering of those who had come to know the Lord. Miss Fenenga and her fellow missionaries must have been thrilled to watch this church structure being built. They had labored in this field for so long to see the fruit of lives being changed for all of eternity. And now these believers had a place of their own where they could gather to pray and to offer praise and hear the Word of the Lord preached on a regular basis. Tirzah, along with her friends and extended family, worshiped in this place right up to the last days of their lives.

We're not sure of all that might have taken place in this building from 1915 forward, but when Thomas and Violet arrived in 1992, they were determined that the gospel would be preached at least one more time within those four walls. Eighty-one-year-old Violet got to work, sweeping the concrete floors, dusting chairs and other furniture. And once the announcement was made, guests were invited, and the time was right—they had church! Attendance was light, but we have no doubt that God was glorified once again in that house of worship.

Thomas preaching at Bethel Church in Midyat, 1992

Before relating the final joyous experience of this trip, it's important to know that from almost the first moment that Thomas surrendered his life to Christ as a teenager, the seed of forgiveness was deeply imbedded in his heart. And obviously there was much for him to forgive.

Having been literally pulled from not just one but two loving homes before he was nine years old, having been indoctrinated in a religion of hate, raised by a father who at best was rough around the edges, being bullied at school, and realizing that all the trauma he had been through in his young life was the result of Islamic jihad, words like *anger* and *bitterness* don't do justice to what his heart must have felt toward those of the Muslim faith. All that baggage made his spiritual transformation that much more remarkable. We can speak with confidence in stating that members of his family, his friends, and the thousands of people he pastored over six decades would agree that his Christlike character was defined by the spirit of gentleness and forgiveness.

We think it can be said that Thomas actually had two goals for this final trip abroad. The first was accomplished when he was able to hold a service in Bethel Church. The second one was accomplished not on Turkish soil but on the plane ride home. Thomas held no bitterness toward those who had brutally ended his mother's life, nor did he hold anger toward the man who had murdered his father. His love for Muslims can be explained only by the transforming work of the Holy Spirit as this final story illustrates.

Once again by God's providence, his seating assignment on the plane placed him beside a Muslim gentleman who was returning to his job at the United Nations building in New York City. For the eight hours of flying time, these two men conversed on numerous topics, but most importantly about their respective religions. Thomas shared his life story and spoke of Christ's love and grace. He sensed that this man was discontent with the religion of his youth and was hungry to know the truth. As the plane approached JFK Airport and at the request of his new friend, Thomas prayed with him to accept Jesus Christ as his Savior! Preaching at Bethel was awesome—but leading this Muslim gentleman to Jesus was priceless!

11

Seasoned Saint

After having served in the Northeast for twenty-five years, Thomas accepted the call to pastor the North Columbus Church of Christ in Christian Union in Columbus, Ohio. He served there from 1964 to 1969. In the 1970s he pastored churches in Evansville, Indiana, and Warren, Michigan. His final transfer was to Heritage Memorial Church in Washington Court House, Ohio, where he served as associate pastor with primary responsibility for the senior adult ministry.

Throughout Thomas's sixty-plus years of pastoring, one area of ministry where he excelled was in caring for the needs of those who hurt. Thomas knew something about pain and suffering and was drawn to those who were sick, facing surgery, contemplating death, or simply discouraged. Chances are, if he wasn't on his knees in prayer or sitting at his desk while studying God's Word, he was most likely at someone's bedside, offering encouragement and hope.

Along with his responsibilities at the church in Washington Court House, he volunteered as chaplain at the local hospital. It was noted at the time of his passing that one of the joys of his final years was making rounds at the hospital, praying with people, mostly strangers, some of whom were dying, and by the power of the Holy Spirit leading them into the assurance of salvation, last-minute rescues as it were, snatching them from the very clutches of the evil one.

On June 17, 1996, without any prolonged suffering, Thomas passed unexpectedly from this life. On the previous day (Sunday) he preached at the church of his son Joe. It was Father's Day, and he chose as his text Matthew 7:11—"If you then, who are evil, know how to give good gifts to your children, how much more will your Father who is in heaven give good things to those who ask Him!" (NKJV). Now being at the age of eighty-five, it was necessary for him to teach from God's Word while seated, and his voice no longer had the strength and volume of youth. Nevertheless, he was in his element almost to his very last breath, doing what he most loved to do: proclaiming the good news of Jesus's love and offer of forgiveness to all who seek Him.

Epilogue

One important takeaway from our father's story is found in the contrast between the decision made by his faithful mother and the one made by his Aunt Medjida, reminiscent of the Old Testament story of Ruth. Ruth chose to follow her mother-in-law Naomi into an unknown future, but a future that was submitted into the hands of Yahweh, the God of Abraham, Isaac, and Jacob.

Orpah, her sister, chose what she thought was the safer and more sensible way, to stay with her people, who happened to be enemies of Yahweh. The Bible tells us what happened to Ruth—she gave birth to the line of David and more importantly, Jesus Christ Himself. According to the Talmud, Orpah died a violent death at the hands of Abishai, King David's general, with no hope of eternal bliss.

Like Ruth and Orpah, Tirzah and Medjida were faced with the most important decision that any of us face in this life—"What will we do with Jesus?" We cannot speak with any authority as to what might have become of Medjida in the years after she denied her faith. We do know that Jesus said, "Whoever denies Me before men, him I will also deny before My Father who is in heaven" (Matthew 10:33 NKJV). We can only hope that she sought the forgiveness and grace of her Creator. Ruth chose well; Tirzah chose well. What has each of us done with Jesus?

In the telling of Thomas's story, we believe he would want us to highlight the legacy of his mother's martyrdom. We should recall the words of Joseph, who said at the end of his life to his brothers, who feared he would seek retribution for all the evil they had done against him, "As for you, you meant evil against me; but God meant it for good" (Genesis 50:20 NKJV). The Kurdish Muslims may indeed have meant evil against Tirzah, but God meant it for good. As a result of Tirzah's tragic death, Thomas in the providence of God landed in America, came to personally know the God of his mother, committed the remaining years of his life to the Lord, and led many into the saving knowledge of Jesus Christ. Seeds planted in the hard soil of Midyat are continuing to bear fruit to this very day in the hearts of many.

There's a second takeaway for me: the ability to forgive and to feel compassion for those who robbed our father of both his mother and his father. That's not natural; it requires something supernatural. We submit that the gentleness, meekness, humility, and supernatural ability to love and forgive those who murdered his parents and other members of his family are the qualities that marked the life of Thomas Hermiz. And he would be the first to say that those characteristics were the direct result of the love and forgiveness of Christ and His ability to transform the damaged and embittered heart of a sixteen-year-old boy headed for disaster.

The cost of following Christ may be different for each one of us, and none of us knows what tomorrow has in store. But He does require that we lay it all down. For Tirzah, that meant giving up her physical life on the earth. It meant giving up her wealth, her husband, and her young children. She counted the cost and decided that Jesus was worth everything. We can't wait to meet her!

Violet and Thomas Hermiz

The photograph on the previous page was taken for the occasion of Thomas and Violet's golden wedding anniversary in May 1985. Friends and family gathered at Heritage Memorial Church in Washington Court House, Ohio, to celebrate fifty years of true love and shared Christian ministry. God brought these two individuals with vastly different backgrounds into relationship with Himself and with each other so they could raise up a family and together serve the body of Christ. To honor our parents on this milestone occasion, our brother Joe and I (John) wrote a song, the lyrics of which follow:

WHAT A LOVE!
By Joe and John Hermiz

Let me sing you a love song
About a love that's oh, so strong.
'Been goin' on for 50 years
Of hopes and dreams, of joys and tears.
Oh, what a love! Oh, what a love!
Now and then when troubles came,
Through it all, love stayed the same.
Oh, what a love! Oh, what a love!

Even before the beginning of time
We know this union was in God's mind.
And every day was written down.
As part of His plan, He blessed them with children,

A LEGACY OF FORGIVENESS

Six little ones they could call their own.
They made a family, made a home.

When there's a need in the family,
She's off the phone, then she's on her knees . . .
"Lord, help Teresa."
"Lord, bless Tom, Ruthie and Mary, Joe and John."
Oh, what a mom! Oh what a mom!
And when we needed someone to look up to,
A pattern for living, a strength to hold onto,
Oh, what a dad! Oh, what a dad!

Even before the beginning of time
We know this union was in God's mind,
And every day was written down.
As part of His plan, He blessed them with children,
Six little ones they could call their own.
They made a family, made a home.

Let me sing you a love song
About a love that's oh, so strong.
'Been goin' on for 50 years
Of hopes and dreams, of joys and tears.
Oh, what a love! Oh what a love!

A LEGACY OF FORGIVENESS

Afterword

By Daniel Hermiz (grandson of Thomas)
Pastor, Darby Grace Church, Plain City, Ohio

These all died in faith, not having received the things promised, but having seen them and greeted them from afar, and having acknowledged that they were strangers and exiles on the earth. For people who speak thus make it clear that they are seeking a homeland.... As it is, they desire a better country, that is, a heavenly one. Therefore God is not ashamed to be called their God, for he has prepared for them a city. (Hebrews 11:13–14, 16)

It has been observed that the sin of the first man caused the second man to murder the third man. What a start to the human story!

Once the crowning achievement of creation (not just good, but *very* good), heaven's ambassadors had become Eden's exiles. Earth's kings had become its tyrants. If any legacy was in sight, surely it was one of destruction and despair. Why? Because humanity had made its choice.

They chose the city of man over the city of God. They chose pride. They chose power and vainglory—they chose death.

Then came a second chance—a third, a fourth, and countless more. Billions of souls later, that tragic choice is still being made. And so we live not in heavenly garden temples but in Babylonian towers. It seems that we walk not in everlasting peace but in endless strife. And upon the observation of these griefs, perhaps we can excuse the cynic for wondering: Is there any hope left for us?

But I like to think that occasionally we hear the echoes of Eden's song. Its glorious melody stirs our hearts while the truth of its lyrics penetrates our minds. It is perhaps nothing less than the master composer's magnum opus, and its libretto of hope is the life-giving announcement of a path back to the great city of God. If *A Legacy of Forgiveness* has a soundtrack, its motif is this song of redemption.

The writer of Hebrews assures us that there is indeed a *better country* (Hebrews 11:16 NIV) and a city *whose architect and builder is God* (Hebrews 11:10 NIV). What's more, we have a great *cloud of witnesses* (Hebrews 12:1 NIV) who have shown us how to get there. That is to say they know the melody of Eden by heart.

Abel was not merely the first victim of man's inhumanity to man. He was the first martyr: *And through his faith, though he died, he still speaks* (Hebrews 11:4). That is to say, he was the first witness to testify that he had seen the promised land! His testimony did not come with a set of blueprints. He didn't paint a picture, write a poem, or sing a song in the literal sense. He simply took God at His

A LEGACY OF FORGIVENESS

Word. Although in that tragic moment he may have lost everything, in reality his sacrifice *still speaks* (Hebrews 11:4) and it was in that same moment that he became the inaugurating member of the cloud of witnesses.

Abel may have been first, but he was by no means the last. The biblical patriarchs were all deeply flawed men. But they, like Abel before them, received the *commendation of God* (1 Corinthians 4:5) because they too took God at His word. They lived (and died) with their hope firmly established not in themselves but in God's plan of redemption.

And so the "cloud" began to grow.

By God's grace, many faithful witnesses would catch glimpses of the great city. *For time would fail me to tell of Gideon, Barak, Samson, Jephthah, of David and Samuel and the prophets—who through faith conquered kingdoms, enforced justice, obtained promises, stopped the mouths of lions, quenched the power of fire, escaped the edge of the sword, were made strong out of weakness, became mighty in war, put foreign armies to flight. Women received back their dead by resurrection* (Hebrews 11:32–35).

Even more would die in faith without such a glimpse. *Some were tortured, refusing to accept release, so that they might rise again to a better life. Others suffered mocking and flogging, and even chains and imprisonment. They were stoned, they were sawn in two, they were killed with the sword. They went about in skins of sheep and goats, destitute, afflicted, mistreated—of whom the world was not worthy—wandering about in deserts and mountains, and in dens and caves of the earth* (Hebrews 11:35–38).

A LEGACY OF FORGIVENESS

On the face of it, the story you have just read is about one family in a specific location, at a particular moment in history. In truth, it is probably a mere paragraph in a long chapter of an even longer epic narrative—the story of how to get to "a better country." May the reader understand, it is not a story about leaving Turkey for the United States. It's a story about leaving behind the city of man and entering the city of God.

And we must not forget that the very Christ who is Himself Zion's King in His desire to bring *many sons to glory* (Hebrews 2:10 NKJV) made an even greater sacrifice to ensure that the great city would one day be occupied by a multitude of the redeemed. So we look to that great cloud of witnesses—Abel, Noah, Abraham, Sarah, the patriarchs, Moses, countless saints of old . . . even my great-grandmother Tirzah. But most important of all, we look *to Jesus, the founder and perfecter of our faith, who for the joy that was set before him endured the cross, despising the shame, and is seated at the right hand of the throne of God* (Hebrews 12:2).

The long arc of history sobers us. While we want to believe tragedy is behind us, we would not be the first to have our hopes of a better world come crashing down. We do not long for death. Nevertheless, we must be ready to suffer—and even to die.

Perhaps that challenge haunts the mind with unpleasant images of gallows, firing squads, guillotines, and many other "mortal ills." Earnestly we pray that such a day never comes for us. And if we are so fortunate to have those prayers answered, a challenge still remains, for the faithful are not called to die once—they are called to *die daily* (1 Corinthians 15:31 KJV).

Surely this is what the apostle Paul had in mind when he pled with Christians, who although spiritual citizens of the heavenly kingdom, had yet to complete their terms as ambassadors to Rome—*present your bodies as a living sacrifice* (Romans 12:1). Sacrifices of course, don't live. By definition they die. So how does a person actually do this? How can someone be a "living sacrifice"?

That, I think, is a question answered and powerfully illustrated in the life of Thomas Hermiz.

As he was unable to escape the horrific images of his childhood, we can imagine how he might have sought to escape such horror in the consuming fire of vapid entertainment, and indeed he started on that path—but that is not the legacy he left.

We would understand if Thomas, a twice-orphaned young boy, chose to isolate himself from people and embrace the life of a lone wolf. But as a wife, six children, and decades of ministry attest—that is not the legacy he left.

Who among us would be surprised if he had been consumed by revenge, being a victim of genocide at the hands of the Muslim Turks? But as one Muslim man providentially seated next to Thomas on his last flight home can attest—that is not the legacy he left.

For Thomas did not take the opportunity to avenge, condemn, or hate. He chose to do the most loving thing a minister of Christ can do: share the hope of the gospel of Christ Jesus, that this man might be saved!

Thomas did not merely sing the song of Eden at one climactic moment. He wove it into the very fabric of his life. In other words, he learned to be a living sacrifice, or to put it in even more sober terms, to *die daily*.

And so by the grace of God we are not lamenting a tragedy—we are celebrating a miraculous victory! As hymn writer Elvina M. Hall so timelessly states it,

> *Lord, now indeed I find*
> *Thy power, and thine alone,*
> *Can change the leper's spots,*
> *And melt the heart of stone.*
> *Jesus paid it all.*

Because of that glorious truth . . . Thomas Hermiz found a better country! He found the city whose architect and builder is God! And as with many who have already joined that great cloud of witnesses, his life "still speaks" to us all these years later. May we run our races in view of that legacy.

He left a legacy not of anger but of mercy.
He left a legacy not of escapism but of transformation.
He did not leave a legacy of despair, cowardice,
 bitterness, or revenge.
He did not leave a legacy of hate.
He left *a legacy of forgiveness*.

Appendix A

Hermiz family tree

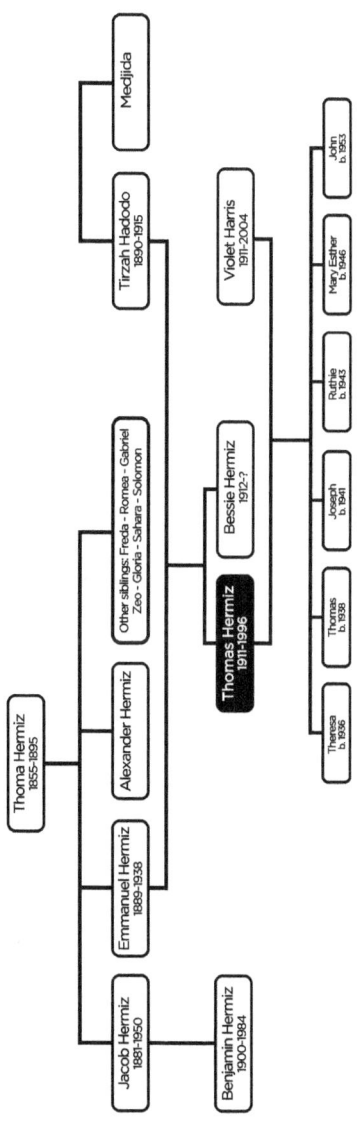

Appendix B

Emmanuel's letter to relatives in Midyat in Arabic
Written September 23, 1928

Emmanuel's letter written on September 23, 1928, translated:

Dear brother Yusuf and Anton, in Midyat,
When you ask me how I am, I am very well. I wish you are also well.
Dear brothers, for more than 10 years, I have not heard from you.
Yesterday I was near Yusuf - uncle of Nebil. I visited Yusuf the son of Sado.
Yusuf told me that Anton married. I have gotten your address from him.
Maybe your heart is not good with me since I haven't gotten a letter in 10 years.

A LEGACY OF FORGIVENESS

Your brother Suleyman and I were close. I have lost a close relative.
Suleyman helped me very much. We were very sincere with each other.
Like I loved Suleyman I love Yusuf and Anton. I want to know how are you?
Thomas every time talks about you. And saying that they helped Thomas very much.
Thomas knows only English so has not written letters to uncles.
He doesn't know any other language. I stay with Thomas in the same room.
We are very good together but we have not contacted our relatives.
I am working in a steel mill and Thomas is thinking about being a pastor.
Thomas said I must give my life to Jesus.
I've been working in the steel mill for 7 years. I learned a job in this mill of iron.
Maybe between 10-20 ton of iron. I like my job. We are very well.

I request for you to tell me about your life.
Please let me know which woman they married and which family the girls came from.
Which children do you have – boys or girls.
Thomas wants very much to know about your life – everything.
I want to learn which men or women are living from side of father and mother after genocide.
I want to know from you the birthday of Thomas and Bessie – the day, month and year.
We had a large Bible and were putting the names and dates inside – it is in the Bible in Midyat.
Please send the Bible.
Please let me know what your job and life is like in Midyat. In which village are you living?
Thomas wants very much to write a letter to you in English if you can translate from English to our language.
I and Thomas want to know how life is in Midyat and the Midyat village.
We send many, many regards to your families.
I kiss the hand of Sado (grandfather of Nebil) and many, many regards to family of Sado.
I send many regards to my Aunt Hane and her son Hanna. Regards to all relatives.
We thank God, Thomas is very, very good. Thomas wants to kiss the hands of Yusuf and Anton.
I want you to have a very good life. Amen.

Your son-in-law
Emmanuel

When you send me the date of Thomas and Bessie please send the old date – Greek Calendar.

A LEGACY OF FORGIVENESS

Appendix C

Hotel Shmayaa's advertisement

Shmayaa Invites You to Mesopotamia...

Shmayaa Hotel, is a magnificent mansion, which has been dwelling at the Assyrian district for 1600 years, located in Midyat, the most prominent ancient city of Mesopotamia where different religions and cultures meet. It has been built by the Assyrian Hirmiz Family from Mosul who paid a gold coin for each stone embroidered with ornaments. This mansion, which has been an authentic witness of a long history, is used as a military headquarters between 1915 and 1930. It has been brought to Midyat district by Bedri Sincar in 2002 and restored by keeping a high fidelity to its original form. Shmayaa Hotel opened its doors for the guests in 2011.

Shmayaa Hotel is 75 km far from Mardin and Batman Airports, and 170 km from Diyarbakir Airport. It is in Assyrian District, just above Midyat Silversmith Bazaar and located in the middle of Churches.

www.ingramcontent.com/pod-product-compliance
Lightning Source LLC
Chambersburg PA
CBHW071136090426
42736CB00012B/2133